THE

GRAMMAR OF PROPHECY.

THE
GRAMMAR OF PROPHECY:

An Attempt to Discover the Method Underlying the Prophetic Scriptures.

BY

R. B. GIRDLESTONE, M.A.,

Hon. Canon of Christ Church, and formerly Principal of Wycliffe Hall, Oxford.

PUBLISHERS
Eugene, Oregon

Wipf and Stock Publishers
199 W 8th Ave, Suite 3
Eugene, OR 97401

Grammar of Prophecy
An Attempt to Discover the Method Underlying the Prophetic Scriptures
By Girdleston, R.B.
ISBN: 1-59244-814-3
Publication date 8/26/2004
Previously published by Eyre and Spottiswoode, 1901

PREFACE.

THE word Prophecy is used in the following pages in the sense of prediction, that is, the utterance of the Divine Purpose, whether such Purpose be declared by direct personal communications, or through angelic visitants, through the medium of dreams, or through visions. The word is by no means necessarily confined to this sense in Scripture; it sometimes signifies forth-speaking rather than fore-speaking, and exposition or personal application of truths already revealed rather than the declaration of definite purposes. But it is this last which is now to be brought under discussion.

The prophecies dealt with are those contained in the Scriptures, *i.e.* the Canonical Books of the Old and New Testaments. No attempt is made to discuss those which can be traced to other sources, if such there be, or to deal with Jewish and early Christian Apocalyptic literature.

The Books of Scripture are taken as a faithful Record, their traditional dates, relative positions and authorship being regarded as trustworthy in the main, though calling for modification here and there, and their text being taken as sufficiently exact for the present purpose.

A "grammar" represents the method which underlies a language. Where there is no method there can be no grammar. If a method can be detected in the prophetic utterances as a whole, we are certainly losers if we do not make use of it. Perhaps the neglect of the study of prophetic method is one secret of the great variety of opinions amongst students of prophecy; and it may account for the fact that so many have given up the subject in despair.

The injury which has come through the rashness of interpreters is very serious. I here refer specially to those who publish and lecture on unfulfilled prophecy in an omniscient style, and who sometimes are in danger of pandering to the popular desire for excitement. This class of prophecy needs no comment.

Other students have been more cautious. It was natural that G. S. Faber, to whom younger students owe so much, should make the Papacy close in 1866. He started from the decree of the Emperor Phocas giving universal sovereignty to the Bishop of Rome in A.D. 606. To this date he added 1,260 years, which brought him to 1866. Frere, another most thoughtful and helpful writer, considered, on somewhat similar grounds, that in 1847 the Mohammedans would be converted, and that in 1867 all the world would be brought to Christ.

In 1840 Pierre Louis, of Paris, calculated that the

end of the world would be in 1900. He added 1,260 years to the date of the capture of the Holy City by Omar (A.D. 636), and this brought him to 1896, at which date he thought that the Jews would return, and he allowed three and a half years for subsequent events. A similar view was taken by a certain L. Evans, on the same grounds, in or about the year 1717, when he modestly wrote his thoughts on the flyleaf of his Bible. After bringing out the date 1896 he continues, "near or about which time the Jews will be reinstated in their own country and city again, which will be at or about one hundred and seventy-nine years hence."

It is natural that each age and country should see itself figuring largely in history, and the men who are conspicuous in its eyes are looked for in the prophetic page. Hence we understand the position which Bonaparte occupied in the mind of students during the first half of the nineteenth century. Similarly, turning from the sphere of wars and politics to that of religion, it would be strange if Protestants did not see the Papacy and the Reformation in the calendar of Prophecy, and equally strange if the marvellous rise and success of Islam, and the thraldom which it has exercised and still wields over the East had been passed by unnoticed in the prophetic record. Certainly these three powers, Bonapartism, Romanism, and Mohammedanism, have laid themselves out for notice, and have, by their utterances, made the path of identification easy to the prophetic student. Each in his turn has claimed to be the representative and mouthpiece of God or of Providence, and the voice of each has been regarded by a vast following as the voice of a god and not of a man. Commentators, therefore, can hardly be blamed if they have seen in the first the resuscitated Beast, in the second the Woman of the Apocalypse, and in the third the Eastern " little Horn " of Daniel.

The danger is lest we become fascinated with a theory, and (as Dr. Anderson has well said in his *Coming Prince*) turn it into a hobby. We are then liable to shut our eyes both to the difficulties attendant on our own view and to the claims of outlying departments in the prophetic word. What we cannot explain we ignore or explain away, and so we do an injury to the cause of Truth. It may be safely laid down as an axiom that the longer we refrain from formulating a detailed programme of the future, and the more time and thought we give to the patient study of the sacred text, the better.

It only remains to mention some of the books on prophetic subjects which I have found specially instructive during a long course of years. Must I apologise for the fact that most of them were written a considerable time ago, and are in English? At any rate they have stimulated thought on the prophetic element in Scripture, and for this, if for nothing else, I owe them a debt of gratitude.

John Davison's *Discourses on Prophecy, its Structure, Use, and Inspiration*, would appear to be still the best introduction to the method of prediction as a whole. Alongside of these discourses should be mentioned Bishop Butler's weighty utterances in the *Analogy*, part II. chap. 7. Patrick Fairbairn's *Prophecy Viewed in Respect to its Distinctive Nature, its Special Function, and Proper Interpretation*, gives the philosophy of prophecy, but tends to spiritualise more than seems legitimate. R. Fleming's *Rise and Fall of the Papacy* (1698) is profoundly interesting. He was a minister of the Scots church in London, and was a keen student of Scripture and of History. His work was republished by Knight in 1849. Renewed attention had been called to the book owing to the fact that the writer had anticipated the fall of the Bourbon dynasty, of which he said, "I do humbly suppose that it will come to its highest pitch about the year 1717, and that it will run out about 1794." On chronological grounds he puts the end of the present dispensation at circ. A.D. 2000, and allowed 1,000 years for the Day of Judgment. Speaking generally, he regards prophecy as a key to the past, and as indicating the completion of History in the future.

Other notable and suggestive works are Sir Isaac Newton's *Observations on Daniel*; the *Dissertations* of Thomas Newton, Bishop of Bristol; James Hatley Frere's *Combined View;* Elliott's *Horæ Apocalypticæ*, which, in spite of all its dogmatism, is a masterpiece of research, and will repay the study of those who discard and resent many of its interpretations; the writings of Professor Birks; the stimulating sermons of Bishop Horsley and (later) of Dr. Arnold; nor should

Pusey's lectures on *Daniel* be passed by. The once-popular works of Dr. Cumming, and the various futuristic studies of such writers as Capel Molyneux and Hugh McNeile, together with the more advanced writings of George Stanley Faber and Edward Irving, are now almost forgotten, but they have helped to keep alive certain definite expectations, and have not been written in vain. Edward Irving's translation of *The Coming of Messiah in Glory and Majesty*, nominally by Ben Ezra, but really by a Spanish Jesuit named Lacunza, has left its mark on many minds, English and foreign.

Later on we reach Dr. Giffard's *Voices of the Prophets*, Payne Smith's *Bampton Lectures*, Guers' *Israel in the Last Days*, Garratt's *Commentary on the Revelation;* also Guinness's *Approaching End of the Age*, which is based on Elliott, but goes further into chronological questions. His *Light for the Last Days* follows, and should be read in connexion with Birks' latest summary, called *Thoughts on Sacred Prophecy*.

On the Messianic subject thanks are specially due to Professor Vincent Stanton's *Jewish and Christian Messiah*. On the post-Millennial kingdom of Christ G. F. Trench has opened out new views, considerably extending the period of Messianic supremacy. With regard to what is beyond, special mention must be made of Isaac Taylor's *Physical Theory of Another Life*, together with the latter part of the *Unseen Universe*, by Professors Balfour Stewart and Tait; also an astronomer's view of *Our Celestial Home*, by Professor Porter, of the Cincinnati Observatory.

For the theory that the English are the Lost Tribes of Israel, reference may be made to *British-Israel Truth*, published by the British-Israel Association, and to a cleverly written book called *The Fulness of the Nations*, by Dr. Alder Smith. As a sample of the way in which Scripture is dealt with by those who hold this theory, I take a test passage, "Go rather to the lost sheep of the house of Israel" (Matt. 10. 6), which this writer thinks inapplicable to the Jews, who have never been lost; hence he would lead us to the conclusion that it points to a mission from the Galileans to the British! But he ignores the first part of the sentence, "*Go not* into the way of the Gentiles, and into any city of the Samaritans enter ye not"; from which words we plainly gather that the contrast is between Israel and the Gentiles, not between Israel and the Jews. With regard to the expression "lost sheep," the writer had only to go back to Matt. 9. 36 to read of the multitudes who fainted and were scattered abroad as sheep having no shepherd. Those who hold the Anglo-Israel theory have done good service by calling attention to the covenant-word *Israel* as a larger word than *Jew* (*i.e.* Judean); but they put themselves out of court by running into the opposite extreme, and practically excluding the Jew from the promises made to Israel, and by ignoring the plain fact that a remnant of the Ten Tribes became permanently combined with the Two after the age of Hezekiah.

PREFACE.

On the resurrection of nations as such the (anonymous) works of the late Mr. Dunn, formerly Secretary of the British and Foreign School Society, especially *The Destiny of the Human Race*, should be consulted. Mr. Edward Grinfield's work * on the Gentile Dispensation collects and discusses the various passages in Scripture which exhibit favourably the case of outside nations, but it does not deal fully with Prophecy.

That a necessity exists for some such book as is now offered as a *Grammar of Prophecy*, may be illustrated from some words lately written by one who is no mean authority on Biblical subjects: "The phenomenon of prophecy (says Professor Margoliouth †) is one which is at present scarcely understood; it belongs to a class of experiences which are not yet brought into the region of science, though it is conceivable that they may be. The words used by the prophets to describe their experiences imply that they were not ordinary; that they were bestowed only on particular individuals; and that they were often falsely claimed by persons who did not really entertain them. The process, therefore, by which the ostensible results of these experiences are denuded of their supernatural character and treated as ordinary utterances is only scientific if the profession of the prophets be shown to be false, *e.g.* if the scene described in Isai. 6 be shown to have been either a delusion or a dishonest

---

* Mr. Grinfield is better known in connexion with his plea for the study of the Septuagint, for which he founded a lectureship in Oxford.

† *Lines of Defence of the Biblical Revelation*, p. 136.

invention. How this can be demonstrated is not obvious; but until it is demonstrated, the assumption that such experiences must be delusions is to be classed with the theory that nature abhors a vacuum, or with the belief that the orbits of the planets must of necessity be circular. Such assumptions may lead to the writing of books, but they are not *science*."

After all, these words are but an echo of those uttered by Lord Bacon in his *Advancement of Learning*,* where he desiderates a treatise in which "every prophecy of the Scripture be sorted with the event fulfilling the same throughout the ages of the world, both for the better confirmation of faith, and for the better illumination of the Church touching those parts of prophecies which are yet unfulfilled; allowing, nevertheless, that latitude which is agreeable and familiar unto Divine prophecies; being of the nature of their Author, with whom a thousand years are but as one day; and therefore are not fulfilled punctually at once, but have springing and germinant accomplishment throughout many ages, though the height or fulness of them may refer to some one age. This is a work which I find deficient; but it is to be done with wisdom, sobriety, and reverence, or not at all."

---

* Ed. Pickering, p. 119.

CONTENTS.

CHAPTER	PAGE
I. Ideas concerning God involved in Prophecy	1
II. Phenomena of Biblical Prediction	8
III. Tests of the Truth of Prophecy	16
IV. Prophecies conditional and unconditional	25
V. The Prophets: their Gifts and their Position	31
VI. The Prophetic Call, and the extent of the Prophetic Period	41
VII. Prophetic Forms of Thought	48
VIII. Recurrent Prophetic Formulæ	54
IX. The Future expressed in Terms of the Past	66
Note on "the Son of David"	73
X. The Predictive Element in the Sacrificial System	76
XI. The Prophetic use of Names	81
XII. The N.T. View of O.T. Prophecy	84
XIII. Chronological Prophecies	89
Note on the Jewish Year	101
XIV. Methods of studying Prophecy	104
Note on the Structure of the Apocalypse	110
XV. Promises to Abraham and David fulfilled in Christ	115
XVI. The Ten Tribes	125
XVII. Israel's Future	134
XVIII. The Parousia and the Millennium	141
XIX. Christ and Antichrist	150
XX. The Final Judgment and that which is beyond	159
XXI. Concluding Observations	170
Leading Dates referred to in Discussions on Prophecy	181
Index of Names and Subjects	183
Index of Texts	186

THE
GRAMMAR OF PROPHECY.

CHAPTER I.

IDEAS CONCERNING GOD INVOLVED IN PROPHECY.

AN ideal Biblical prophecy may be expected to have the following characteristics:— *An ideal prophecy.*

i. It plainly foretells things to come, and is not clothed in the ambiguities which we observe in heathen oracles and vaticinations.

ii. It is designed and intended to be a prediction, and is not like the suggestion of Caiaphas, which might be called an unwitting prophecy.

iii. It is written, published, or proclaimed before the event to which it refers, and which could not be foreseen at the time by ordinary human sagacity.

iv. It is subsequently fulfilled in accordance with the original utterance, due regard being had to the recognised laws of prophetic speech and interpretation.

v. It does not work out its own fulfilment, but stands as a witness until after the event has taken place.

vi. It is not an isolated utterance, but is more or less clearly correlated with other prophecies, and is practically one of a long series of predictions.

These are the marks of an ideal prophecy. It is manifest, however, that many Biblical prophecies do not come up to the ideal; but some of them will be found to do so, notably those that have to do with the destiny of the seed of Abraham, and with the mission of the Son of God. In the latter case it might be objected that the Lord Jesus deliberately set Himself to fulfil the prophecies; and this is freely granted, so far as He Himself is concerned. But, on the other hand, those who forsook Him, falsely accused Him, smote Him, spat upon Him, crucified Him, cast lots on His vesture, pierced His side, but left His bones unbroken, had not the slightest idea that they were fulfilling what was written. They did it in ignorance; and God overruled their folly and wickedness so as to fulfil what He declared beforehand by the mouth of all the prophets that the Messiah should suffer (see Acts **3**. 17, 18). This public testimony of St. Peter is confirmed by St. Paul, who pointed out to the Jews in the synagogue of Antioch that the inhabitants of Jerusalem and their rulers, in their ignorance of the Lord and of the voices of the prophets, which were read out in their synagogue every Sabbath, fulfilled them in condemning Him (Acts **13**. 27).

Prophecy a method of revelation. Taking it for granted that the six points named above exhibit what an ideal prophecy ought to be, we have to consider how far the existence of such a prophetic element in Scripture is *a priori* conceivable or inconceivable. There is a strong tendency in some writers to reduce Biblical prediction to a *minimum*, if not to do away with it altogether, the object being to smooth away the difficulties which lie in the path of unbelievers, and to make some elements of Christianity more accessible to those who stumble at the idea of anything supernatural. But the predictive element in the Bible cannot lightly be disposed of. It is distinctly claimed by the writers themselves. Isaiah challenges heathenism to produce its prophecies:—"Let them shew us what shall happen ... shew the things that are to come hereafter, that we may know that ye are gods" (Isai. **41**. 22, 23). He claims prediction as an attribute of God Himself:—"I am God, and there is none like Me, declaring the end from the beginning, and from ancient times the things that are not yet done, saying, My counsel shall stand, and I will do all My pleasure ... I have spoken, I will also bring it to pass: I have purposed, I will also do it (Isai. **46**. 9–11). The Prophet Amos goes so far as to say that the revelation of the Divine purpose was normal:—"Surely the Lord God will do nothing without revealing His secrets to His servants the prophets" (Amos **3**. 7). Similar passages can be produced from both the Old and New Testaments. Thoughtful students of these books thus find themselves compelled to take the Biblical predictions as they stand, reading them inductively and dealing with them on a large scale. Manifestly they are not wholesale forgeries; nor are they a series of happy guesses; but they must be regarded as the unfolding of purposes which were revealed at sundry times and in divers manners, and were only realised in history ages after they were uttered, whilst some are still waiting for their fulfilment. The prophetic element is thus not only a proof, but also a method of Revelation.

What then are the ideas concerning God which are implied in the series of literary phenomena which make up Biblical prediction?

1. The *Personality* of God lies at the foundation of this as of all else. God is not a dead force, but a living Father. He is not only the uncaused spring of all secondary causes, but a Being possessed of consciousness, *i.e.* of something akin to our consciousness, inclusive both of feeling, whether of pleasure and displeasure, and of will. The fact of our own

Personality of God.

personality leads us on purely rational grounds to ascribe personal existence to the Father of our spirits. The Personality of God may be—must be—infinitely greater than ours: it is eternal; it needs not to be nursed and trained through the medium of a body; it is something essential and fixed, but not impassive and hard. The grand words, I AM THAT I AM, stand like a monument of the Divine personality, and commend themselves to the searcher after truth as the basis of all other existence, and as the starting-point of all sound investigation into such a discussion as lies before us.

Eternity of God.

2. The *eternity* of God is a necessary corollary. As nothing preceded Him and brought Him into being, so nothing can cause His existence to waste away or be obliterated. He was: He is: He is to come. Whilst human beings are creeping round the circumference of Time, He remains as the eternal centre, the same yesterday, and to-day, and for ever. From His throne in the spirit world He looks down on His creatures, and in one glance beholds their beginning, their course, their consummation. A thousand years do not affect Him in the sense in which they affect us. The lapse of ages will not change His moral and spiritual attributes. The tendency to create and, if need be, to save, must be His through all time and through all space.

Divine purpose.

3. The existence of *purpose** in the Divine mind follows next. He is "wonderful in counsel." Purpose springs from Tendency, and is formulated in Plan. These are human words, but they point to something in the Divine nature, and the thought concerning them is freely expressed in Scripture, *e.g.* by Isaiah and St. Paul. It is here that Revelation becomes

---

* In the Old Testament various words are translated "purpose." Some signify "speech," others "thought" or "good pleasure."

specially necessary. Our knowledge of God's attributes (which after all is infinitesimal) would not enable us to predict His purposes. We could only tell what their qualities would be. But "known unto God are all His works from the beginning of the world" (Acts 15. 18). Every step in creation, in origination, in differentiation, whether in our planet or in the stellar and spiritual universe, is best worded by us as the result of mental or spiritual action on the part of God. Some things may be directly ordered and executed by what we usually call physical force, as when He said "Let there be light," and there was light; others, especially where moral beings are concerned, are permitted, aided, and inspired, rather than compelled; but our reason and moral sense lead us to believe that in the long run these permissions, and the results which follow—even though apparently failures—will be turned to account in the direction of the original intention and design. Human beings are always making plans, whether in politics, in military matters, in construction, or in games. We are forecasting every day and all day long. This is one element in our likeness to God.

4. The Divine *omnipotence* is the fourth element. He is able to carry out His purposes. "Hath He said, and shall He not do it? Hath He spoken, and shall He not make it good?" When we call God "Almighty," we mean that His spiritual and (in a secondary sense) His physical powers are not restricted by human limitations or by the unforeseen. Nothing is impossible with Him, provided always that it is consistent with His attributes and purposes. The hearts of kings are in His rule and governance. Men may think they are carrying out their own will, when really they are His agents. We read of the Assyrian, "I will send him . . . I will give him a charge . . . howbeit he meaneth not so,

Divine omnipotence.

neither doth his heart think so; but it is in his heart to destroy and cut off nations not a few" (Isai. **10**. 6, 7). "Him, being given up by the deliberate counsel and foreknowledge of God, ye have taken and by wicked hands have crucified and slain" (Acts **2**. 23). This is what we mean by Providence. It is the utilisation of existing forces, physical, human, angelic, to carry out the Divine purposes. There are many links, some large and some small, in the chain, but the hand that makes and holds it is Divine. When we consider the power of our own will on matter and on mind, we recognise that He in Whom we live and move and have our being must have some power akin to ours, only infinite and perfect.

Divine self-manifestation.

5. He is *capable of making known His purposes beforehand.* That the Divine Being, who has endued us with so many avenues of communication with each other, should have debarred Himself from all such means, is an idea which carries with it its own refutation. We are taught that man was originally made in the Divine image that he might be God's child, and we gather consequently that Divine intercourse with human beings was normal before the Fall. But now what used to be natural has become supernatural. God ordinarily hides Himself, but reveals Himself when it is needful. In our present condition we should be dazzled and bewildered and rendered unfit for our ordinary duties if God walked amongst us as He did in the Garden of Eden. Hence it is that reserve in the Divine communications with man is reasonable and natural, and has become the rule rather than the exception. That reserve, however, is not absolute. Just as we depart from our ordinary routine under special circumstances, so there is nothing unreasonable in the unveiling of the Divine purpose to the eye of special persons, or even

nations, where God sees fit. The mission of the Son of God, together with all that led up to it, and all that follows from it, is the most conspicuous of all the reasons which justify such an unveiling. Divine Intervention thus furnishes the *rationale* of Divine Revelation. The two ran side by side through the preparatory ages which closed with the return from the Captivity. A gap of some four centuries succeeded. Then came the fulness of time; and Revelation and Intervention were re-awakened in the manifestation of the Lord Jesus Christ, in the outpouring of the Spirit, and in the first preaching and recording of Christian truth.

Such are the ideas of God which are involved in the theory of Biblical prediction: His Personality, His Eternity, His Purpose, His Providence, His Revelation. Are they not reasonable? What sort of a God would He be who was deprived of these attributes, or was debarred from expressing them in action? Certainly He would not be the God of the Jew or of the Christian. He would not be such an ideal God as Reason and Feeling suggest. In fact, He would in some respects be less godlike than an ordinary man. Let the student of human nature face these reflections fully and fairly. He will then at least acknowledge that no theoretical objections to prediction *per se* need hinder him from studying the prophecies contained in the Scripture.

CHAPTER II.

PHENOMENA OF BIBLICAL PREDICTION.

Number of prophecies.

HAVING shown cause for believing that there is nothing unreasonable in the idea of prediction regarded as the unfolding of a Divine purpose, it will be best to take a bird's-eye view of the phenomena presented by Biblical predictions as a whole. The following points seem the most noteworthy :—

1. *Their number and distribution.*—They are by no means confined to the so-called Prophetic Books. In fact, there is hardly a book in the Bible which is wholly devoid of the prophetic element. Putting aside frequent utterances of promise and threat, and proverbial expressions which indicate the downfall of wickedness and the success of righteousness in the long run, we find numerous definite predictions running through the Pentateuch, Joshua, Samuel, Kings, Chronicles, the Psalms and Prophets, the Gospels and Acts, the Epistles to the Romans, Corinthians, Thessalonians, the Epistles of St. Peter, St. John, and St. Jude, and the Book of the Revelation. They are to be numbered not by tens but by hundreds, and are constantly coming to the front in the course of a series of Books which extend over a period of at least 1,500 years. Moreover, those prophets whose writings we possess are only a few out of many; and they themselves must have uttered many more predictions than those which have come down to us.

Variety of subjects.

2. *The variety of their subject matter.*—They have to do with individuals, as in the case of Lamech's prophecy concerning Noah, or the utterance of the man of God at Bethel concerning Josiah; with tribes and families, as in the case of Noah's prediction concerning Shem, Ham, and Japheth,

or of Jacob's blessing on his twelve sons; with the rise and fall of empires, as in Nebuchadnezzar's dream; with the destiny of the earth, as in the Second Epistle of St. Peter; with the coming and work of the Redeemer, as in the prophecy concerning Bethlehem in the Book of Micah; with His glorious reappearing, as in the angelic message recorded in the 1st of Acts; with the resurrection of the saints, as in 1 Cor. 15; and with the final Judgment of the Race, as in Rev. 20.

Nothing seems too great and nothing too small for the prophetic spirit; nothing too near, and nothing too far off; nothing too secular, and nothing too sacred. The birth of a child, the death of a king, the shortening or prolongation of a life, the discovery and punishment of a sin, the inroad of a nation, the preservation of a family, the advent of a Redeemer, the destruction of a planet—all find their place in Biblical prediction.

3. *The individuality of the speakers and writers.*—While there are certain characteristics more or less common to all prophetic utterances, the Spirit of God by no means prompted them all to speak in the same style or to treat their subject in the same method. Each prophet preserves his individuality and exhibits a certain independence of thought and language. Peculiar lines of thought and feeling spring out of the circumstances in which the various writers are placed. Thus, David's peculiar position as an anointed but persecuted king makes him unconsciously a type of Christ, and his strange experiences enabled him to give expression to feelings far deeper than his own. The same may be said of Jeremiah. Besides this, each period had its special needs which the prophets were called to supply; and every man of God contributed what was required for his own day, all being under the direction of the Master mind, and each contributing unwittingly for the benefit of future ages.

Personal characteristics.

10   GRAMMAR OF PROPHECY.

Relationship of Books.

4. *Their unity and relationship.*—Although Biblical prophecies are the utterances of many men and the product of many ages, yet when regarded as a whole they are found to be correlated. They form a vast series which extends through many generations. There is a main line of prediction, and there are divers branches. The terminus or objective of the main line in the Old Testament is the coming of the Messiah. And the terminus of New Testament prophecy—all uttered and written down *after* His coming—is the coming again of the Messiah. Thus, "Testimony to Jesus is the spirit of prophecy" (Rev. 19. 10). Side-issues must be read in connexion with this main line. The eternal God breathes through all the utterances, whether great or small, whether central or subsidiary. Each prophet contributes unwittingly to a complete programme, whilst each has his own special style and office. The later prophets frequently take up the earlier predictions, and re-issue them with certain additions or modifications. Moses takes up the blessing of Jacob: Jeremiah brings out afresh the words of Isaiah and his contemporaries: the Lord Jesus carries forward the utterances of Daniel: the Apocalypse projects into the future the unfulfilled residuum of Old Testament prophecy.

The more critically we examine the Books the more we are struck with the proofs that the later writers were well acquainted with the literary remains of their predecessors and contemporaries. They had free access to the archives and registries in which such writings were kept, and there were guilds of scribes who were expert in copying MSS. See, *e.g.* Judg. 5. 14; 1 Kings 4. 3; 1 Chron. 2. 55. Inspiration does not imply originality, and prophets borrowed freely from one another without mentioning the fact. When we compare Micah with Isaiah, Jeremiah with almost all previous writers, Zephaniah with Isaiah, Haggai with Ezekiel, and St. Jude with St. Peter, we cannot fail to detect this spiritual communism among the prophets.

Besides this, there are in the Bible traces of a prophetic scheme or cycle in accordance with which sacred history proceeds. It comes to light in Lev. **26**, and again in Deut. **26—29**, and culminates in the national Song preserved to us in Deut. **32**, which all Israel had to learn by heart. This Song contains their history in short. The people are regarded (i.) as thriving, (ii.) as forgetting God, (iii.) as suffering for their sin, (iv.) as appealing for help. Their God looks down upon them, and (i.) is jealous for His people, (ii.) redeems them, (iii.) punishes their enemies, (iv.) incorporates some of the outside nations with His rejoicing people. Verbal quotations from these chapters named above abound in the Psalms and the prophets; they are observable in the time of the Maccabees, *e.g.* in 2 Macc. **7**. **6**, where we read, "Moses in his Song declared He shall be comforted in His servants"; also in the New Testament seven or eight utterances of the Song are reproduced.* In the prophets the cycle usually takes this form:—Ingratitude, Idolatry, Punishment, the call to Conversion, the promise of Restitution, the Judgment on persecuting nations, Jerusalem the centre of all nations.

5. *The predictive element is entwined with the historical.*— *Prophecy and History.* Prophecy and Providence run together; and prediction, speaking generally, is to be found in a biographical or historical setting. It is not always easy to disentangle the one from the other, for both grow together. If Pharaoh had not dreamed his strange dreams, and if Joseph had not interpreted the cup-bearer's dream, the course of Israelitish history might have run differently. The promises made to Abraham became the *magna charta* of his seed. They are appealed

---

* See the *Student's Deuteronomy* (Eyre and Spottiswoode), where the leading quotations are given in full.

12   GRAMMAR OF PROPHECY.

to as the ground of Divine intervention throughout the Pentateuch and in the later Books, and again by Ezra after the Babylonian Captivity. They emerge afresh in the New Testament at the time of the birth of Christ, whose coming is considered their fulfilment.

Effect of Prophecy.

6. *The predictive element is generally subservient to the practical and spiritual.*—The object of prophecy was not to excite surprise, but to stimulate enterprise. It was not a narcotic or a substitute for action, but was designed to provoke to love and good works. The prophet's business was to warn men, to kindle hope in their breasts, and to turn them to God. There is no room for fatalism in the Bible. However near or however sure a prediction might be, it was intended to call out faith, and faith was to call out action; and if the day of action was allowed to slip by without being used, then the prophecy was in vain. The promises concerning Canaan incited Israel to fight, not to sit still. When David found by enquiring of God that the men of Keilah would deliver him into Saul's hands, he did not sit still and let himself be captured; he fled away. Isaiah's message to Hezekiah telling him that he should die prompted him to pray that he might live; and he did live.

How far the prophecies produced the full effect which was intended may well be questioned. The word often fell on dull ears and hard hearts. The predominant tone of warning which is so characteristic in the pages of Jeremiah and Ezekiel caused men to feel as Ahab did towards Micaiah—"I hate him, for that he doth not prophesy good concerning me, but evil." Still, whether they heard or whether they forbore, they knew that God had spoken. The burning of Jeremiah's roll was probably unique, though it has had plenty of imitators in later days. Some seed, at any rate, fell on good ground. In the 3rd chapter of Micah, after a review of

Judah's sin, the prophet says, "Zion shall be ploughed as a field, and Jerusalem shall become heaps, and the mountain of the House as the high places of the forest." Did this definite threat produce any effect on the people? We know that it did. A century later we find the matter referred to by the elders of the land, who say that the effect was that Hezekiah "feared the Lord and besought the Lord, and the Lord repented Him of the evil which He had pronounced against them." See Jer. **26**. 17–19.

7. Another remarkable feature of prophetic diction is that *its language at first sight looks extremely exaggerated.* It is in truth thoroughly oriental, and if the Bible had been originally written in English and by Englishmen, it would doubtless have been worded very differently. Even in such a sober book as the Epistle to the Colossians (**1**. 23), we are told that the Gospel had been "preached to every creature under heaven," as if the injunction of Mark **16**. 15 had already been carried out. A hundred times destruction is threatened in the most terrible forms against Israel and against other nations, and yet it arrives in a very reduced form. It is evident that neither desolation nor destruction were final or complete. Look, for example, at Isai. **24**. 18–20:— *[margin: Hyperbole of Prophecy.]*

> "He who fleeth from the noise of the fear shall fall into the pit;
> And he that cometh up out of the midst of the pit shall be taken in the snare;
> For the windows from on high are open,
> And the foundations of the earth do shake.
> The earth is utterly broken down;
> The earth is clean dissolved.
> The earth is moved exceedingly;
> The earth shall reel to and fro like a drunkard,
> And shall be removed like a cottage;
> And the transgression thereof shall be heavy upon it;
> And it shall fall and not rise again."

It is needless to multiply such passages as these which the prophetic Books supply so freely. They naturally suggest two thoughts. First, if threats which can be tested in this world are not fulfilled to the letter, how will it be with regard to those which affect the world to come? And secondly, if punishments are not fully carried out, how will it be with rewards?

The wording of the Books inclines us to believe that we have presented to us what may be called extreme cases and ideal judgments, which are often considerably modified in practice. They enshrine the laws of Divine government in their most telling forms; and in this sense they may be compared with the teaching of the Lord Jesus Himself as preserved in the Gospels.

It must not be forgotten that terms of comparison in Hebrew are more pointed than in English, and transitions are far more abrupt. This is true in ordinary narrative, and of course it affects prophecy still more. When we read such sentences as "Your cities are burnt with fire," "Incense is an abomination to me," "Your hands are full of blood," "Every one loveth gifts" (Isai. **1.** 7, 13, 15, 23), we quite understand that we must deduct something for Hebrew style; but we neglect the application of this principle to other passages which need it quite as much, *e.g.* some of the utterances of our Lord and His apostles. When we read of a slave, "He shall serve his master for ever" (Exod. **21.** 6), we know that conditions are sure to arise which will snap that permanent bond; for service closes at death. Similarly, when we read of God's land that "The forts and towers shall be for dens for ever" (Isai. **32.** 14), we know that the continuance of the desolation here implied will come to an end, for the very next verse points to Restitution—"*Until* the Spirit be poured upon us," etc. We have, in a word, to compare passage with passage, thought with thought, and truth with truth, and even then we can only speak modestly concerning predictions which are clothed in the most extreme language.

Our Authorised and Revised Versions have added to our difficulty instead of removing it; for they frequently translate the Hebrew duplication by the word "utterly," where the sense requires the word "surely." Thus in Gen. 2. 17 they render the passage rightly, "Thou shalt surely die"; but in Deut. 4. 26, "Ye shall soon utterly perish . . . ye shall utterly be destroyed." This class of rendering is a serious misfortune.

CHAPTER III.

TESTS OF THE TRUTH OF PROPHECY.

Fulfilment of Prophecy.

THE first test of the truth of a prediction is its fulfilment. When Jeremiah confronted the false prophet Hananiah and gave an ironical "Amen" to his sanguine but fictitious message, he added these words, "The prophet which prophesieth of peace, when the word of the prophet shall come to pass then shall the prophet be known that the Lord hath truly sent him" (Jer. **28**. 9). The word is thus confirmed and established; and whilst the fulfilment attests the prediction, the fact that there was a deliberate prediction by an authorised person marks the event as something intentional and as part of a Divine purpose. Our Lord said, "Now I have told you before it come to pass that when it is come to pass ye might believe" (John **14**. 29; comp. chap. **13**. 19).

Viewing the Bible as a whole and as a trustworthy collection of writings, we are driven to the conclusion that hundreds of prophecies have been fulfilled; and we are thus led to believe that in cases where the fulfilment is not recorded we may be satisfied that they, too, came true, with the qualifications referred to in the previous chapter. Some prophetic utterances must be in process of fulfilment at the present time, whether in personal experience, or in the history of the professing church, or in the movements of nations, or in the silent preparation of the earth for its next great change. The time for some has not yet come; but when we take the Books approximately at their traditional dates, we find that so many predictions concerning Israel and

TESTS OF THE TRUTH OF PROPHECY.

concerning the mission of Christ have been already verified, that we feel assured as to the future. History will yet put its seal on the remaining prophecies, and it will be true in the time to come, as it has been in the past, that God's word does not return to Him void.

2. But this criterion of prophecy does not stand alone. *Faith in God.* We can readily see that something more was needed in order to persuade men that the things uttered would surely come to pass. Above all things there must be faith in God. "I believe God (says St. Paul) that it shall be even as it was told me" (Acts 27. 25). God is by the necessity of His own nature faithful and true. His word stands for ever. He calls us to be faithful because He is faithful. If we refuse to believe Him we are sinning against one of the deepest laws of our nature. When once we have reason to believe that God has spoken, we have nothing to do but to believe.

3. Again, we must be sure of the man or the medium *True and false prophets.* through whom the Divine message reaches us. If we throw ourselves back into the Israelite age we see the necessity of this. If a prophet was a well-known person whose authority was established, as in the case of Samuel, Isaiah, or Paul, his word would be taken by those who knew him without hesitation; otherwise perplexity might arise. Many predictions referred to the far future, and the minds of men might remain in suspense for many generations if no prophecy could be regarded as certain until the event verified it. Moreover, even the fulfilment of a prophecy might not be an absolute proof that it had come from God. It is quite conceivable that the utterances of some of the false prophets, who formed such a perplexing element in Israelite life, might come true. Thus, additional assistance was needed for the confirmation of the faith of the original hearers of sacred predictions.

Accordingly there was a provision of signs and tokens, miraculous or providential, which were to be regarded as attestations of the messenger and consequently of his message. These signs were of two classes. There were signs preceding and signs following.

Signs preceding.
When Moses was sent to speak to the Israelites concerning their approaching deliverance from Egypt and concerning his own mission as their leader, he asked how it should be known that God had sent him. The answer affords us the first instance of miracles wrought by the hand of man—and it is noteworthy, by the way, that we have no record of such miracles in this sense in the antediluvian and patriarchal ages, a fact which is strongly in favour of the trustworthiness and antiquity of the Book of Genesis. The turning of the rod into a serpent and the other signs were so many attestations that Moses was sent by God and that His word must be trusted and obeyed. As we saw in a former chapter that the Divine intervention in the Person of the Son of God was the *rationale* of revelation, so we see that the mission of the Prophets gives the *rationale* of the miraculous.

The word "miraculous" is here used in a wide and popular sense. No one can say where nature ends, and where that which is not nature begins. The more we pursue nature the greater and more subtle does it become. There is, however, a normal order of events and conditions, and there is an abnormal. Some of the signs or miracles recorded in Scripture range themselves under the first of these titles and may be considered as Providential, *i.e.* as divinely arranged coincidences, *e.g.* the condition of the Red Sea and of the Jordan when Israel crossed them. Others are distinctly abnormal or extraordinary. These must be studied as a series, not as isolated marvels. They were effected through Divine wisdom and power either in order to guarantee the prophet, or to symbolise and signify something about the mission of the Son of God. The word "miracle" is used only six times in the Old Testament (A.V.). It stands for two Hebrew words, one of which (מופת) is generally translated "wonder," and signifies a portent; whilst the other (אות) means "a sign," and occurs as far back as Gen. 1. 14. Neither of these words draws a distinction between nature and the supernatural. The three words used in the New Testament distinguish between a sign ($\sigma\eta\mu\epsilon\tilde{\iota}o\nu$), a marvel or portent ($\tau\epsilon\rho\alpha\varsigma$), and an exhibition of force ($\delta\dot{\upsilon}\nu\alpha\mu\iota\varsigma$).

We gather from Scripture that whilst sacred revelations in vision* and otherwise ran through the course of history in a direct line from Adam to Moses alongside of a series of Providential circumstances, including answers to prayer, the wonderful works, which we call miraculous, kept step with the mission of the prophets both in the Old Testament and in the New. The signs (to use St. John's favourite word) which the Lord Jesus wrought were the guarantee that He was at least a prophet, and so they called men's attention to His words. They were, indeed, more than this, but this was their first object.

A notable instance of a sign preceding the event is given us in 1 Kings 13. A man of God is sent to Bethel to predict the coming and mission of a certain king who should be named Josiah. But the fulfilment of the prediction was delayed for two centuries. Accordingly, in order to give a guarantee that the words spoken would surely come to pass, two signs are granted. First, the altar was rent there and then and the ashes poured out; secondly, the king's hand was first withered and then restored. The sign granted to

---

* The sign sought by Abraham (Gen. 15. 8) was not a miracle wrought by the hand of man, nor was it an attestation to others that Abraham was a prophet; it was simply a vision granted to him for the confirmation of his faith.

20 GRAMMAR OF PROPHECY.

Hezekiah is in the memory of all, though we in these days hardly know how it was accomplished. In the New Testament a notable case is that of Zechariah, whose faith in the astonishing revelation made to him sadly needed confirming. His dumbness was a sign before the event, and his sudden recovery of speech may be taken as a sign which followed after.

Signs following.

The demand of a sign was often made, and naturally enough, during our Lord's mission. Certainly plenty of signs were vouchsafed to His generation. Many of them accompanied His teaching, and were both illustrative of it and subsidiary to it; but the most notable answer which He gave to the demand for a sign was what He more than once referred to as the sign of the Prophet Jonah; in other words His resurrection on the third day. This must be considered as a sign which was fulfilled in what followed after that critical day of His betrayal, crucifixion, death, and burial. The outpouring of the Holy Spirit is regarded by St. Peter in a similar sense. The Lord was to baptize with the Holy Ghost; and when the Spirit was shed forth it was regarded as a sign that Jesus was indeed exalted. Similar "signs following" are traceable in other parts of the Bible.

In Exod. 3. 12, we read, "This shall be a sign that I have sent thee: when thou hast brought forth the people out of Egypt ye shall serve God upon this mountain." Certainly nothing was less likely than that Israel when on their journey from Egypt to Canaan should work their way round by Horeb. Consequently, when this actually happened, Moses would have his faith in God's mission confirmed. Again, when Isaiah proclaimed deliverance to Hezekiah and his people, he said, "This shall be a sign unto thee: ye shall eat this year such things as grow of themselves, and in the second year that which springeth of the same." The actual deliver-

TESTS OF THE TRUTH OF PROPHECY.

ance was on the very night in which these words were uttered, but the sign reached onwards into the second year. Perhaps the celebrated sign given to Ahaz (Isai. 7. 14) is to be read in a similar sense. When the king had refused to ask a sign that he should be delivered from his enemies, God gave him a sign which was not to be fulfilled for seven centuries—"Behold, a virgin shall conceive and bear a son." The Great Redemption by the virgin-born Saviour was a sign that God was with man, and confirmed the conviction that all the lesser and earlier deliverances granted to the line of David (of which Ahaz was one) were foreshadowings of His gracious and supreme act of intervention in the Person of the virgin-born Son.

These signs, whether preceding or following, are to be regarded as part of the Divine method of revelation, and they were specially adapted to confirm the faith of those who beheld them or knew of them.

4. Yet another provision was made to confirm men's faith in utterances which had regard to the far future. It frequently happened that prophets who had to speak of such things were also commissioned to predict other things which would shortly come to pass; and the verification of these latter predictions in their own day and generation justified men in believing the other utterances which pointed to a more distant time. The one was practically a "sign" of the other, and if the one proved true the other might be trusted. Thus, the birth of Isaac under the most unlikely circumstances would help Abraham to believe that in his seed all the families of the earth should be blessed. The fact that Shebna was degraded from the office of grand vizier, and Eliakim put in his place, tended to establish Isaiah's position as a prophet (see Isai. 22. 15 and 36. 3). Jeremiah publicly warned Hananiah that he should die within the year, and he did so (Jer. 28. 16, 17);

Prophetic foreground.

and the event would confirm Jeremiah's authority in the eyes of the people. There are many similar cases in the Old Testament and in the Acts of the Apostles.

But the two classes of prophecy thus referred to were frequently combined in one; they were, in fact, so intertwined that it is almost impossible for the student to disentangle them. They read as a whole, the parts being related as the foreground and the background of a landscape, or as two pictures in a dissolving view. Writers on prophecy have usually pointed out this oft-recurring phenomenon; and some critics have gone so far as to say that wherever there is a background there must be a foreground; that the far future, if predicted at all, is only shadowed forth vaguely in expressions which have to do with the prophet's own day: whilst others go a step further and suggest that the mission of the prophet is only to exhibit the spiritual side of the time then present, whether as a warning or an encouragement, in view of future possibilities.

These ideas can hardly be sustained in view of the facts recorded in Scripture, on which alone we have to depend for our materials. But it cannot be doubted that the intertwining of the near and the distant is a common characteristic of prophecy, and that it largely contributed to the confirmation of men's faith in the prophetic word. In Isaiah and his contemporaries the notable deliverance of Hezekiah and his people from the hand of Sennacherib is associated with a greater deliverance which was not accomplished until seven centuries later; and the Return from Babylonian captivity is interwoven with brilliant pictures of an Israelite Restitution which has not yet been accomplished (see, *e.g.* Micah, chaps. **4** and **5**). Our Lord's prophetic utterances (Matt. **24** and **25**) begin in the time then present, but merge into scenes still future, and commentators are not always of one mind as to where the overlapping takes place. The prophecies of Daniel concerning "the abomination of desolation" seemed to be fulfilled in the time of Antiochus Epiphanes. This we see from 1 Macc. **1.** 51, where we read that "in the fifteenth day of the month Chisleu, in the one hundred and forty-fifth year (*i.e.* circ. B.C. 168), they set up the abomination of desolation upon the altar," etc. But our Lord, speaking 200 years later, tells his disciples that some of them would see it in their own days, and gives them instructions as to what they were to do when they saw it: "When ye shall see the abomination of desolation spoken of by Daniel the prophet stand in the holy place, then let them which be in Judea flee into the mountains," etc. (Matt. **24.** 15).

5. The case of the false prophet was provided against in another way. These men, deceiving and being deceived through many ages, were actuated by various motives, of which Baalism (Jer. **2.** 8), the love of money, and even the love of drink were prominent (Isai. **28.** 7; Mic. **3.** 11). They were banded together in large communities from the days of Ahab onwards, and were specially vigorous and popular in the time of Jeremiah. They reappeared in the Christian Era, and in the last times they will work false miracles, as the magicians did in the time of the Exodus. It was thus necessary that their influence should be taken into consideration and guarded against, both in the law of Moses and in the teaching of Christ. Accordingly we read in Deut. **13.** 1–3, "If there arise among you a prophet or a dreamer and giveth thee a sign or a wonder, and the sign or wonder come to pass, in connexion with which he saith, 'Let us go after other gods and serve them'—thou shalt not hearken unto the words of that prophet or dreamer. For the Lord God is proving you to know whether ye love Him with

Truth, a test of mission.

all your heart." In other words, men were to consider the doctrine as well as the signs, and if men's teaching tended towards Baal-worship or any other form of heathenism, it might be known for certain that they prophesied out of their own spirit, and the Lord had not sent them. Further, our Lord said, " Ye shall know them by their fruits" (Matt. 7. 16). Thus the authority of teaching was to be recognised by the tendency of the life which it produced. The sceptical scoffers referred to by St. Peter and St. Jude walked after their own lusts (2 Pet. 3. 3 ; Jude 18). This was enough to condemn them. St. John gives another simple test whereby the false prophets of his day, probably towards the end of his life, might be discerned. He says, " Believe not every spirit, but test the spirits whether they be of God : because many false prophets are gone out into the world. Hereby know ye the spirit of God : every spirit that confesseth that Jesus Christ is come in the flesh is of God, and every spirit that confesseth not (in other words, that denieth) that Jesus Christ is come in the flesh is not of God : and this is that spirit of antichrist whereof ye have heard that it should come, and even now it is in the world" (1 John 4. 1–3). He is here no doubt referring to the germs of Gnosticism which had already begun to work among the Christians of Western Asia.

It is worth while to note how ready the Lord Jesus was to submit to the tests here mentioned. He submits to be judged by " the law and the testimony " (Isai. 8. 20), and challenges His opponents to convict Him of sin (John 8. 46). There is no break in the unity of doctrine, or in the standard of life, between the Old Testament and the New. The one is the bud, the other is the full flower. Christ came not to destroy, but to fulfil.

CHAPTER IV.

PROPHECIES CONDITIONAL AND UNCONDITIONAL.

AMONG the points bearing on the nature and fulfilment of prophecy, few call for more special attention than this,—that some predictions are conditional, whilst others are absolute. Many of the utterances of Scripture (*e.g.* Lev. 26) present alternative prospects. If Israel followed the course of obedience, certain happy consequences would ensue. If they disobeyed, various specified evils would follow. So it was in the case of individuals. Jeremiah said to King Zedekiah, "If thou wilt go forth to the king of Babylon's princes, then thy soul shall live, and this city shall not be burned with fire; but if thou wilt not go forth to the king of Babylon's princes, then shall this city be given into the hand of the Chaldeans and they shall burn it with fire, and thou shalt not escape out of their hand" (Jer. **38.** 17, 18). Similarly, two alternatives were present before the little remnant with whom Jeremiah found himself associated after the Captivity (Jer. **42.** 10–13). *Conditional prophecies*

But the conditional nature of a prediction is not always plainly stated in Scripture. Thus, Jonah is said to have preached that within forty days Nineveh should be destroyed; the people repented at his preaching, and Nineveh was not destroyed; yet so far as we know, the people were not told that if they repented the judgment should not fall on them.

Predictions of this class are so numerous that we conclude there must have been some unexpressed but underlying condition in all such cases which justified God in departing from the literal fulfilment of the prophetic utterance. What *Repentance affects fulfilment.*

that condition is we may gather from such chapters as Jer. **18** and Ezek. **33**. After Jeremiah had watched the potter at his work and had learned the great lesson of the Sovereignty of God, a further message was presented to him: "At what instant I shall speak concerning a nation and concerning a kingdom to pluck up and to pull down and to destroy it, if that nation against whom I have pronounced turn from their evil, I will repent of the evil that I thought to do unto them. And at what instant I shall speak concerning a nation and concerning a kingdom to build and to plant it, if it do evil in My sight that it obey not My voice, then I will repent of the good wherewith I said I would benefit them" (Jer. **18**. 7-10). Acting on this principle, Jeremiah speaks thus to the princes when the priests and prophets wanted to have him slain:—"The Lord sent me to prophesy against this house and against this city all the words that ye have heard. Therefore now amend your ways and your doings and obey the voice of the Lord your God, and the Lord will repent Him of the evil that He pronounced against you" (Jer. **26**. 12, 13). If the people would repent, in one sense, the Lord would repent, in another. And on what ground? On the ground of the original, essential and eternal attributes of the Divine nature, and on the ground of the old promises and covenants which God had made with the fathers as a result of those attributes. Thus God says to Israel, "Return, thou backsliding Israel, and I will not cause Mine anger to fall upon you, for I am merciful and I will not keep (anger) for ever" (Jer. **3**. 12). It is the goodness of God which leads to repentance (Rom. **2**. 4). Ezekiel's words are most significant:—"When I say to the righteous that he shall surely live, if he trust to his own righteousness and commit iniquity, all his righteousnesses shall not be remembered, but in his iniquity which he hath committed, in it shall he die. Again, when I say unto the wicked, Thou shalt surely die; if he turn from his sin and do judgment and justice . . . he shall surely live" (Ezek. **33**. 13–15). In accordance with this fixed principle the appeal goes forth, "Repent and turn from all your transgressions, so iniquity shall not be your ruin. Cast away from you all your transgressions whereby ye have transgressed, and make you a new heart and a new spirit. For why will ye die, O house of Israel. For I have no pleasure in the death of him that dieth, saith the Lord God; wherefore turn and live ye" (Ezek. **18**. 30–32).

It may be gathered from these and other passages that the actual fulfilment of a prophecy depends on the moral and spiritual condition of those to whom or of whom the word is spoken. This consideration throws light on many things.

It is a fundamental principle of revealed theology that God is slow to anger and repenteth Him of the evil. "He is not slack as some men count slackness, but is longsuffering to us-ward, not willing that any should perish, but that all should come to repentance" (2 Pet. **3**. 9). This principle is exhibited in His dealings with the nations which inhabited the countries round Canaan. Their judgment may have been postponed or modified in consequence of some good thing which was seen in them. Similarly, in the case of individuals we can trace a relaxation or postponement of judgment. When Ahab had been convicted of grievous sin he rent his clothes and put sackcloth upon his flesh and fasted and went softly. "And the word of the Lord came to Elijah, saying, Seest thou how Ahab humbleth himself before Me? Because he humbleth himself before Me I will not bring the evil in his days: in his son's days will I bring the evil upon his house" (1 Kings **21**. 27–29).

Divine and human repentance.

It is probable that hundreds of prophecies, which look absolute as we read them, were not fulfilled in their completeness because the words of warning from the prophet produced some result, even though slight and temporary, on the hearts of the hearers. God does not quench the smoking flax.

It would be interesting to enquire how far the principle thus clearly laid down is applicable to the case of our first parents. God is represented as saying to Adam, "In the day that thou eatest thereof thou shalt surely die" (Gen. **2. 17**). The eternal attribute of goodness lay beneath the utterance; and in this sense, if in no other, the Lamb was regarded as slain before the foundation of the world. So it came to pass that Adam did not actually die when he ate the forbidden fruit, though the seeds of spiritual and physical death were then sown in him.

In Num. **14.** 34 we read, "Ye shall know My breach of promise." The words have to do with the threat of judgment on Israel for their unfaithfulness and their murmuring, in consequence of which their carcases were to fall in the wilderness, and forty years should elapse before they entered Canaan. There is some doubt as to the exact rendering of the Hebrew word תנואה, translated "breach-of-promise." Probably the margin in the A.V. ("the altering of My purpose") comes sufficiently near the truth. It would seem as if there were a constant reconstruction of the Divine plan, to meet the new set of circumstances brought about by human failure; so that whilst in one sense God is not a man that He should repent (Num. **23.** 19 and 1 Sam. **15.** 29), yet He does repent, in the sense of changing His course (1 Sam. **15.** 35).

Unconditional prophecies.

Shall it be said then that all prophetic utterances are conditional? By no means. There are some things concerning which "the Lord hath sworn and will not repent" (Ps. **110**. 4); and it is of supreme importance to find out what they are, so far as they have been revealed. The reduction, postponement, or doing away of privilege and penalty in the case of any specified person or generation, is one thing: the gracious counsel of God towards the children of men as a whole is another. The slow preparation of earth as a habitation for man, with its stores of coal and other treasures which man alone is constituted to enjoy and use, indicates Purpose on a large scale. The nature and possibilities of a human being with all his limitations, failures and inconsistencies, marks him off as having been placed on the border-land of two worlds, the physical and the spiritual. The selection of a man, a family, a nation, to run a course of many generations, inheriting, embodying, and conserving a long line of spiritual communications, is a simple fact of history which cannot be overlooked. Moreover, we find that this leads up to and prepares the way for the realisation of the very grandest conception ever entertained (as far as human knowledge can grasp) by the Author of all good, namely, Redemption. These gifts and this calling of God are without repentance (Rom. **11**. 29). No sin of man, no antagonism, alienation, or indifference, has been permitted to bar the way of God's great purpose in Christ. It is irreversible. The nations may combine against the Lord and against His anointed; but "He that sitteth in the heavens shall laugh; the Lord shall have them in derision. Yet (in spite of all) have I set My Son upon My holy hill of Zion" (Ps. **2**. 4, 6).

These irreversible promises do not depend on man's goodness, but on God's. They are absolute in their fulfilment, even though they may be conditional as to the time and place of their fulfilment. The promise of the seasons recorded in Gen. **8.** 22 is to be true "while the earth remaineth." The promise made to David and his seed was to have no end; that is to say, as long as there was a human race upon earth, so long there should be one of the seed of David to rule (Ps. **89.** 29, 36, 37). The same is the case (in a sense yet to be discussed) with the promise of a permanent "Israelite" seed, with its priests and Levites (Isai. **66.** 20, 21; Jer. **33.** 19–26). Equally sure and unconditional is the promise of the new heavens and the new earth (Isai. **65.** 17; **66.** 22; 2 Pet. **3.** 13; Rev. **21.** 1).

Times and seasons may be modified, days may be shortened, events may be accelerated or delayed, individuals and nations may come within the scope of the promises or may stand outside; but the events themselves are ordered and sure, sealed with God's oath, and guaranteed by His very life.

CHAPTER V.

THE PROPHETS: THEIR GIFTS AND THEIR POSITION.

HITHERTO we have been dealing with the characteristics of prophecy rather than with the character and position of those who were God's mouthpieces. But it is time we should ask, What do they say concerning themselves? and what explanation of the wonderful gift bestowed on them do they offer?

1. As a class they make no pretence to remarkable learning or natural sagacity. We are in the habit of talking of the school or schools of the prophets, but this is not a Biblical expression. There were "companies" of prophets, whose office was choral rather than predictive (see 1 Sam. **19**. 20), and the sons of the prophets were naturally associated both in work and in common life (see 1 Kings **20**. 35; 2 Kings **2**. 3; **4**. 38; **9**. 1). To some extent they formed a guild or caste analogous with the priestly caste, though not necessarily hereditary as in the case of the priests; but this was a mere matter of custom and convenience, and there is no indication that they taught one another the art of prediction. The same may be said of the New Testament prophets. Some of the prophets were undoubtedly men of learning, *e.g.* Moses, Daniel, and Paul; but others, as Amos and Peter, were uncultured. There were plenty of books of magic among the Babylonians and other Eastern nations, but there is no trace of their use by the prophets of the Bible; and at Ephesus the books of those who used "curious arts" were publicly burnt when their owners became Christians.

Prophecy not taught by man.

Prophecy not the result of frenzy.

2. They did not claim animal or mental excitement as the source of their gift. In many respects they present a marked contrast with the Canaanite Baal-prophets, the Greek soothsayers, the African rain-maker, the American medicine-man, the Mohammedan dervish, or the Western spiritualist. It is true that prophecy is largely poetical and raised out of the ordinary style of thought or feeling, and that in some cases the speaker seems to have been in an abnormal state of mind, being rapt or taken out of himself, whether in the body or out of the body he could not tell (2 Pet. **1.** 21 and 2 Cor. **12.** 2). The word translated "trance" in Acts **11.** 5; **22.** 17 is literally "ecstasy," *i.e.* an abnormal condition; but this word does not mean frenzy or excitement. It is used in the Septuagint in Gen. **2.** 21 and **15.** 12 for a deep sleep. So far as we can judge from their writings the men who had the gift of prediction were collected and self-restrained, though earnest, and at times impassioned. The spirits of the prophets were subject to the prophets (1 Cor. **14.** 32); and their body did not act on the mind, but rather the mind on the body.

The association of music with prophecy is referred to more than once in Scripture. Not only did it produce a soothing influence on the perturbed spirit of King Saul, who was himself a prophet in one sense, but we are told that whole companies of prophets went in procession with musical instruments before them (1 Sam. **10.** 5), and Elisha actually sent for a minstrel (*i.e.* a harpist), as if to put himself into a due frame of mind before prophesying (2 Kings **3.** 15). The habit of prophesying upon a harp, *i.e.* praising God with a musical accompaniment, is referred to in 1 Chron. **25.** 1 and Ps. **49.** 4. Music evidently could do a good deal, but it could not supply the knowledge of the future.

It cannot be denied that men of a certain mental stamp, *Natural foresight.*
and perhaps of certain nationalities, are more gifted than
others in the matter of insight and foresight. The old world
and the new, the most cultivated and the most uncivilized
of nations, have had their oracles, soothsayers, augurs, astrologers, prognosticators, horoscopists, and such like. We
cannot dismiss presentiment and second-sight as a childish
imposture. It may be that coming events do cast their
shadows before, and that some persons have skill to detect
the signs of the future, where ordinary people are too dull to
observe them. There are elements in human nature of which
we know very little. The well-known French astronomer,
M. Flammarion, has entered fully and seriously into this
question, and has produced the result of many years' enquiry
in his late work entitled *L'inconnu*. In this book an attempt
is made to found a scientific theory on an induction of
instances; but it is closed with an honest acknowledgment
that no theory can yet be arrived at. Andrew Lang's work
on *The Origin of Religion* compares the gifts and ways of
barbarous people with those of our own country in such
matters as divining and crystal-gazing, and shows that the
savage and the civilized have similar tendencies. Remarkable
and well-attested instances of horoscopes are given us by
Colonel Meadows Taylor in his *Story of My Life* (p. 228, etc.).
The fact that the unauthorised attempts to obtain knowledge
and influence through this class of agency are branded in
Scripture as infamous, by no means leads us to dismiss them
as mere jugglery.*

3. The universal testimony of Scripture is that the gift *Divine inspiration.*
of true prophecy was from the God of Truth. Strong
pressure was exercised on the mind of the prophet, but it

---

* On the Hebrew terminology connected with the subject see *Old Testament Synonyms* (Nisbet), chap. 26.

was from within (*i.e.* from the spirit-world), not from without. So we read in Neh. **9.** 30, "God testified by His Spirit in His prophets"; compare Zech. **7.** 12, where we read of "The words which the Lord of Hosts hath sent in His Spirit by the former prophets." So (Heb. **1.** 1) "God spoke unto the fathers in the prophets," and they were "moved (or borne along) by the Holy Ghost" (2 Pet. **1.** 21). Prophecy was thus a normal method of divine agency for the utterance of Truth.

4. Further light as to the nature of the prophetic gift is obtained by an examination of the leading Hebrew terms and expressions used in connexion with the subject.*

It is remarkable that none of the names for a prophet signify either pre-vision or pre-diction. All rather point to communications from the spirit-world prompting to the utterance of what is felt or seen.

Hebrew names.

The ordinary word for a prophet is *Nabi* (נביא), which in Assyrian signifies one who proclaimed the will of the gods. A *nabi* was a "medium" between God and man, and so a spokesman. The position may be illustrated from some analogous cases. When Moses shrank from the work committed to him, God said, "Thou shalt speak unto Aaron and put words in his mouth, ... and he shall be thy spokesman unto the people; and he shall be unto thee instead of a mouth, and thou shalt be to him instead of God" (Exod. **4.** 15, 16). Again, "I have made thee a god to Pharaoh, and Aaron thy brother shall be thy prophet" (Exod. **7.** 1).

The second name for a prophet is *Roeh* (ראה), which exactly answers to the word "seer," *i.e.* one who sees with the natural eye. We gather from 1 Sam. **9.** 9 that this was

---

* See *Synonyms of the Old Testament*, chap. 20. The English word "prophet" is simply a reproduction of the Greek προφήτης.

THE PROPHETS: THEIR GIFTS AND POSITION. 35

the word in popular use in Samuel's early life. It was, however, never used in the early books, and is by no means a common word, being almost confined to the Chronicles, where it is used of Samuel and Hanani. It occurs in Isai. **30.** 10, and nowhere else in the prophetic books.

The third word is *Chozeh* (חזה), one who sees with the mental eye, or, to use a modern term, a clairvoyant. Though the verb is used of spiritual vision as far back as Exod. **24.** 11 and Num. **24.** 4, the noun is first used in its technical sense in 2 Sam. **24.** 11 of David's seer.

In 1 Chron. **29.** 29 all three words are used together, and we learn from the passage that men of this class had a notable function. They were historians. Samuel the seer, Nathan the prophet, and Gad the clairvoyant wrote certain books which we have practically in the Books of Samuel.* *Modes of Divine speech.*

The inner voice reached the mind of the prophet under three conditions. He might be spoken to in his wakeful hours, as when Isaiah was stopped while walking across a court and sent back with a message to Hezekiah (2 Kings **20.** 4). A message might come to him in a dream, as in the case of Joseph the son of Jacob, or it might be presented to his mind's eye in a vision. We read in Num. **12.** 6, "If there be a prophet among you, I the Lord will make Myself known to him in a vision and will speak to him in a dream." These two methods of revelation are contrasted with the communications which God made to Moses, which were more direct: "With him I will speak mouth to mouth, even apparently (*i.e.* visibly) and not in dark speeches (or riddles); and the likeness of the Lord shall he behold" (*v.* 8). The likeness of the Lord must have been One who was in some respects human and in some respects Divine; in fact, it must

---

* See *Deuterographs*, Introduction, (Oxford University Press).

have been the Person who is sometimes called the Lord, sometimes the Angel or Agent of the Lord, sometimes the Archangel or the Captain of the Lord's host, and sometimes the Word of the Lord.

A dream might come to anyone as a warning or suggestion, but a vision was granted to special persons, such as Ezekiel or St. John. When such a vision was presented to the mind's eye, heaven seemed to be opened and the spirit-world disclosed to view. The objects presented might be familiar, as an almond tree or an altar, or they might be strange combinations, as in the case of the cherubim, or there might be manifestations of the Divine Being too dazzling and sublime to be put into words. In the case of a long and elaborate vision, or series of visions, it is not always easy to determine what portions are contemporary and what consecutive. The trance (*i.e.* transit or crossing from the physical sphere to the spiritual) might be short, as in the instance of Micaiah (1 Kings **22.** 19), or it might extend—practically, if not consciously—over some time (see *e.g.* Ezek. **40—48** or Rev. **1—22**).

The process of prophetic rapture is set forth by various expressions, *e.g.* "I saw," "I heard a voice behind me," "the word of the Lord came," "the Lord spake to me with a strong hand." The voice seemed within (see Hos. **1.** 2, "the beginning of the Word of the Lord *in* (בְּ) Hosea"). It was like a burden laid on the spirit of the prophet (Isai. **13.** 1; Mal. **1.** 1), and he was bound to utter it in the right time and place. In fact he could not do otherwise, though he might resist for a time (Jer. **20.** 9).

Such is the account given by the prophets themselves of the phenomenon to which they were subjected. It invites study. It challenges comparison with any long series of utterances to be found in other countries and in connexion with other religions, if such can be found. But as a matter of fact any attempt at comparison will evince itself as contrast.

5. With regard to the social position and occupations of the prophets little need be said. They were not confined to one Tribe, though the priestly family contributed largely to their number. They were probably men of middle class, though not all on one level. They were not above labouring with their hands when necessary, as in the case of Elisha, Amos, and St. Paul, though they mixed freely with kings, princes, priests, and people, and with foreigners. Some of them occupied a more conspicuous position than others owing to circumstances, being the poets, historians, and preachers of the nation. They were probably a substitute for the priests in the Northern Kingdom, and a supplement to them in the Southern. Though not always under the direct movement of the prophetic spirit, they might at any time be called upon either by God directly, or by the needs of the occasion. Some of them led, and perhaps framed, the prayers and praises of the people; others expounded the Law, convicted, rebuked, and preached righteousness, whilst others were scribes, conserving, copying, and compiling the Scriptures. David had a "seer" who was almost like a private chaplain to him. So it was with other kings; and throughout the history we find them frequently intervening in times of emergency and calamity.

Social and moral position of prophets.

After all, they were men of like passions with us (Acts 14. 15; Jas. 5. 17). We have no reason to regard them as free from ordinary temptations or from serious wrong doing. They had no general grant of omniscience or infallibility in things sacred and secular. The gift that was in them was apparently limited to certain seasons and subjects; and when they had no message they were left morally and intellectually to the ordinary powers of human nature. It has often been discussed whether their authority on secular matters was as high as when God's truth was concerned. This much at any rate must be granted, that the special quickening of their memory and other powers through the inspiration of the Holy Ghost would give a unique value to their testimony on matters which had in any way come under their own cognisance.*

Prophetesses.

It should be added that both sexes were capable of receiving the gift. This is plain with regard to the general or non-technical use of the word in such chapters as Joel **2**, Acts **2**, and 1 Cor. **14**. But further, we have the case of Huldah in the Old Testament and of Anna (*i.e.* Hannah) in the New. Isaiah's wife is called a prophetess (Isai. **8**. 3), perhaps because she was the wife of a prophet, but she may have had a gift like that of Deborah.

Prophetic understanding.

6. The question is sometimes raised, How far did the prophets understand the full import of their own words? In answering it, we have to avoid two extremes. They were not omniscient; but they were messengers. As such it was by no means necessary that they should be able to fathom the full meaning of the words entrusted to them. Were they, then, simply on a level with their hearers? This was hardly true in all cases. A prophet who beheld a vision had permission at times to question the being with whom he was in communication. See for examples Zech. **4**. 4–7, and Rev. **7**. 13, 14. Similarly, a definite though enigmatical solution of prophetic truth was given to Daniel (**12**. 8, 13). The words of St. Peter (1 Pet. **1**. 10–12) are most instructive. In dealing with the subject of salvation, he tells us that the prophets sought and searched diligently what manner of time the Spirit of Christ which was in them pointed to, when it testified

---

* See Dr. Gifford's Fourth Lecture in *The Voices of the Prophets* (Edinburgh, 1874).

beforehand the sufferings which should befall the Messiah and the glories which should follow. The apostle here refers to the class of passages which the Lord Jesus expounded after His Resurrection (Luke 24. 26, 46). The apostles themselves wanted to know these things (Matt. 24. 3; Acts 1. 6); and it was natural that the earlier prophets should do so. St. Peter, however, continues that it was revealed to these prophets that the things they announced had not to do with their own time, but with a later period which culminated at the time of the outpouring of the Spirit.

The conclusion seems to be that the prophets were generally ahead of their age, and that whilst the hearers and first readers saw little beyond an immediate and national fulfilment, the prophets themselves knew that the foreground of their prophecy was only of secondary importance, and that the background was international, spiritual, and redemptive.

7. There is yet one more point to be added about the prophets. *Depth of conviction* We have every reason to believe that they were honest men who were ready to suffer and, if need be, to die for the cause of God and His truth. They knew in Whom they had believed. They had been called and commissioned by God, sometimes in a startling way. A great responsibility was thus thrown upon them. If God called them to speak, woe to them if they kept silence. "The lion hath roared: who will not fear? The Lord God hath spoken: who can but prophesy?" (see Amos 3. 8). No diffidence, no lack of eloquence, no defect in personal aspect, no fear of man, must hinder a Moses, a Jeremiah, an Ezekiel, a Paul, from a free utterance of the Divine message. They had to face mockery, persecution, imprisonment, and even death, for the truth's sake. The story of the prophets of the Old and New Testaments is a story of martyrdom in both senses of the word. Little of it is told in Scripture because the Sacred Books came

to us from these very men. But we have enough. The closing chapter of the Chronicles, some passages in Jeremiah, the solemn words of the Lord Jesus (Luke **11**. 50, 51), the burning utterances of St. Stephen, and the 11th of the Hebrews, tell us all we want to know. The men whose words we are considering were heroes. They were the salt of the earth, from the days of righteous Abel to the time of Zachariah, and from the days of John the Baptist till the close of the prophetic period, the course of the prophets was stained with their own blood.

These men were not impostors, forgers, fraudulent scribes, ushering in their private views under cover of great names such as Moses or Isaiah. They spoke and wrote under a sense of responsibility. They were commissioned from on high, and their words were words of truth.

CHAPTER VI.

THE PROPHETIC CALL, AND THE EXTENT OF THE PROPHETIC PERIOD.

THE raising up of the prophets, and fitting them and calling them to their work, is a subject replete with interest, but need only be briefly treated here.

1. In many cases we can glean nothing about the early life of the prophets or about their call to the prophetic office. How little we know of Enoch; but he stands out as a unique figure in the pages of sacred history. The case of Abraham is very different. We gather from later parts of his story that he had frequent communications with the Most High, some of which were appearances like those subsequently vouchsafed to Moses. His was a call to action rather than to speech. He was not a preacher, but an heir of certain promises which involved him in special responsibilities. Joseph was a dreamer from his youth, and soon recognised that dreams might enshrine messages from God. He, like Abraham, was called to action, that he might preserve life. Accordingly, the Latin Vulgate translated his Egyptian name by the title *Salvator mundi* (comp. Gen. **41**. 45; **45**. 7; **50**. 20). Moses was an old man when he received his final call, but there can be little doubt that he had been previously stirred, through providential circumstances, to take a saving interest in his people. Samuel was a child when the voice sounded so clearly in his ear that he thought it was Eli who was calling him,

The Divine call.

but the boy was ready. Elisha was engaged in ploughing when Elijah threw his mantle over him, but he understood the signal. Doubtless God had prepared him. Daniel was a youth, perhaps not more than thirteen, when he became one of a little band of total abstainers from polluted food and drink. His call to become an interpreter soon followed, and his story presents many points of analogy with that of Joseph. Isaiah must have been quite young when he saw his first vision, for he probably lived on into the reign of Manasseh, whose captivity in Babylon supplied the foreground for the greater captivity (2 Chron. **33**. 11), Jeremiah felt himself a mere child when the Word of the Lord came to him. Ezekiel was in his 30th year when his eyes were opened to behold visions. Amos was following the flock when the Lord took him and told him to prophesy. John the Baptist, like Jeremiah, was marked out for special work before he was born. The same was the case with St. Paul (Gal. **1**. 15), though the conscious call to Christian service was much later.

In every case which we have specified, the call can be traced, not to personal ambition, but to Divine influence, and usually to the sound of an inner voice. It was not a matter of gradual education. The unwitting preparation might be long, but the call to act or speak was sudden. It did not come after a series of failures, but sprang into being full-grown.

The age of Prophecy.

2. Reviewing the subject historically, we are led to enquire when the prophetic spirit first showed itself. According to the Biblical narrative, our first parents had free communication with Him by whose *fiat* they had been brought into existence. Abel's faith and righteousness, to which such striking reference is made in the New Testament, may have

been fostered by messages from the Most High. We have no reason to believe that Enoch was the first of the prophets. The "sons of God" may have been a prophetic line. The patriarchal period was prophetic; then followed waves of prophetic energy in accordance with the needs of Israel. At some times prophets were numerous, at others the gift was in abeyance. When Samuel was a child the Word of God was precious or scarce; subsequently it flowed in a narrow stream until a period which extends from the reign of King Uzziah onwards. When Old Testament history closes, *i.e.* 400 years before Christ, the prophetic spirit waned. There were no prophets in the Maccabean period, which began about 150 B.C., and the Books of the Old Testament seem to have been regarded as a complete collection 100 years earlier (see 1 Macc. **4.** 46; **9.** 27; **14.** 41; Ecclus. prologue). According to the Jewish tradition deliberately affirmed by Josephus in his controversial work against Apion (i. 8), the prophetic Scriptures were closed in the time of Artaxerxes, *i.e.* in the days of Nehemiah and Malachi. At last the 400 years of silence that followed came to an end, and the spirit of prophecy reasserted itself at the time of the birth of John the Baptist and of the Lord Jesus. In the Pentecostal Age there was a great outflow of prophecy, both in the wider and narrower sense, as the Acts and Epistles testify.

If it is difficult to fix the beginning of prophecy, so it is with regard to its end. When the generation which succeeded that of the Apostles died out (circ. A.D. 150), the gift was waning, if not actually expiring. There might still be special cases of insight and foresight. There were men and women whose faith was strong, and whose prayers were specially effectual, so that signs and wonders were wrought by their hands. But well-attested instances become

Post-apostolic Prophecy.

rare. The fostering care needed by the infant Church seems to have been gradually withdrawn, and Christian communities and individuals were left to the more ordinary influences of the Holy Spirit. No books were regarded as authoritative except those that left the hand of the Apostles and Prophets, on whom the Church was founded, and of whom St. John was probably one of the last. By general though not universal agreement, these Books stood alone. It is true that the early Church had its Montanists, and in later times there have been Mystics, Quakers, and others who have protested against the imposition of too narrow a limit on the working of the prophetic Spirit. This protest we are bound to respect; but for practical purposes we have good reason for believing that the main body of truth outlined in the New Testament is a sufficient guide to life, and that any attempt to supersede the Scriptures will land us in formidable difficulties. The Holy Spirit operates still, but not in the same way, perhaps even not to the same extent, as of old.

Chain of prophets.

3. It may be well before closing this chapter to exhibit in outline the chain of prophetic men to whom reference is made in Scripture. Doubtless there were many others whose names are not recorded, and perhaps some may have been accidentally omitted from the lists. The men in question had the gift of prophecy in the wider sense, though the power to predict may not have been given to all.

The list of the Prophets may be classified and arranged as follows:—

A. *In the Antediluvian Age* (Gen. 2—9) we may detect a line of prophetic influence from Adam onwards through Enoch, Lamech, and Noah.

B. *In the Patriarchal Age* (Gen. 11—50) the gift comes

THE PROPHETIC CALL, AND THE PROPHETIC PERIOD. 45

out in the history of Abraham, Isaac, Jacob, and Joseph. Enquiry of the Lord is first referred to in Gen. **25.** 22.

C. *In the Mosaic Age* we have Moses himself. The seventy who "prophesied" probably had no special gift of prediction. The Urim and Thummim are established; and enquiry of God is carried on, apparently in the sense of learning the path of duty (Exod. **17.** 15). Joshua was a prophet in the sense of being in direct communication with God (Josh. **5.** 14.; see also **6.** 27).

D. *In the Age of the Judges* enquiry of the Lord was frequent (chaps. **1.** 1; **18.** 5; **20.** 18, 27). We read of the angel of the Lord appearing (chap. **2.** 1, 20), of a prophet in the time of Gideon (**6.** 8), of a divine message in the time of Jephthah (**10.** 11), and of an angel or man of God in the time of Samson's parents (**13.** 6). Samson was probably contemporary with Eli.

E. *In the Age of Samuel and the United Kingdom*, Hannah, Samuel's mother, may be regarded as a prophetess; a man of God is referred to in 1 Sam. **2.** 27; Samuel becomes a prophet (chap. **3.**), and is regarded through the Old and New Testaments as the head of the Prophetic Order. Enquiry of the Lord was frequent in those days. David himself was a prophet of special stamp, as we can gather from the Psalms and from the references to them in the Gospels and also in the Acts (see **2.** 30). Nathan and Gad were also prophets in those days, and united with Samuel in providing the materials for the history of David's reign; whilst Nathan, Ahijah, and Iddo did the same for Solomon (see 1 Chron. **29.** 29, 30; 2 Chron. **9.** 29). They also had to do with the arrangement of the musical services in their time (2 Chron. **29.** 25).

F. *The Divided Kingdom.*—Rehoboam's biographers were Shemaiah and Iddo (2 Chron. **12.** 15). Abijah's biographer was Iddo. Jehoshaphat's life was written by Jehu the son of Hanani (2 Chron. **20.** 34) ; Uzziah's and Hezekiah's by Isaiah (2 Chron. **26.** 22 ; **32.** 32) ; Manasseh's were in the chronicles of the Seers (2 Chron. **33.** 19); and Jeremiah probably had to do with the history of the later kings (see 2 Chron. **35.** 25 ; **36.** 12, 21). This illustrates the fact that the Old Testament historians were prophetic men. All the way through this period prophets were found in both kingdoms. Thus, Ahijah the Shilonite and Shemaiah have to do with Jeroboam as well as with Rehoboam (1 Kings **11.** 29 ; **12.** 15 ; **15.** 29), and the man of God crosses from the Southern Kingdom into the Northern (1 Kings **13**). Jehu the son of Hanani has to do not only with Jehoshaphat, but with Baasha (1 Kings **16.** 1, 7, 12). There are other prophets of that period, viz. Oded and his son Azariah (2 Chron. **15.** 1, 8), also the prophet mentioned in 1 Kings **20.** 13-23, a man of God in *v.* 28, a son of the prophets in *v.* 35, and Micaiah in chap. **22.** 8. The period covered by Elijah and Elisha is thus ushered in, together with the prophecies of Jahaziel (2 Chron. **20.** 14), Eliezer the Morasthite (2 Chron. **20.** 37), and another Jehu (2 Kings **10.** 30 ; **15.** 12). It must not be forgotten that Elijah not only spoke, but wrote (2 Chron. **21.** 12). We thus come down to the age of Joash, when there were prophets (2 Chron. **24.** 19), including Zechariah the son of Jehoiada (2 Chron. **24.** 20), whilst Jonah is said to have written to Jeroboam II. of Israel (2 Kings **14.** 25). In Amaziah's time there was a man of God and a prophet (2 Chron. **25.** 7, 15). We thus reach the galaxy of prophets—Amos, Isaiah, Hosea, Micah, and perhaps Joel ; we have also Zechariah's vision (2 Chron. **26.** 5), and the words of Oded to Pekah (2 Chron. **28.** 9). In Josiah's time and the closing years of the Kingdom we have Huldah, Zephaniah,

Jeremiah, Ezekiel, and Daniel; whilst later on we have Haggai and Zechariah, and Malachi closes the prophetic period of the Old Testament.

Reviewing the list, we find a chain of prophetic speakers and writers covering the whole period from Samuel to Malachi. With regard to the earlier ages our materials are not sufficient to enable us to complete the chain, but indications point to the probability that Prophecy was granted at all critical stages of human history.

CHAPTER VII.

PROPHETIC FORMS OF THOUGHT.

Figurative language of Prophecy.   THAT which makes the language of prophecy so vivid and yet so difficult is that it is always more or less figurative. It is poetry rather than prose. It abounds in peculiar words and expressions which are not usually to be found in prose writings of the same date. It is rich with allusions to contemporary life and to past history, some of which are decidedly obscure. The actions recorded in it are sometimes symbolical, sometimes typical. The present, the past, and the future, the declaratory and the predictive, are all combined and fused into one. The course of individuals, the rise and fall of nations, the prospects of the world at large, are all rapidly pourtrayed in realistic language.

As we read we ask ourselves whether the figures which thus pass over the page in such quick succession are to be interpreted literally or ideally. How much are we to deduct as oriental and Israelite? and what of the *residuum*? When God said to Jeremiah (6. 26), "Gird thee with sackcloth," did the prophet go and put it on? Was Ezekiel really carried to Jerusalem by a lock of his hair (Ezek. 8. 3)? Did Hosea actually marry an abandoned woman? The best way of dealing with all these questions and others of the same class is the inductive method. Treat the passages as members of a series or parts of a body of Truth, and interpret them accordingly.

Let us begin by taking certain words which are constantly recurring in prophecy.

PROPHETIC FORMS OF THOUGHT.

1. One of our first difficulties lies in the simple word "EARTH." Does it usually stand in prophecy for the land of Israel? or for the whole world? The Hebrew word leaves the matter open, for it is equally applicable to either. Take, for example, the opening of Isai. **24**, "Behold, the Lord maketh the earth empty." At first sight we are inclined to take the English word in its widest sense; but after a detailed examination of the chapter we fall back on the more restricted sense; and yet we feel that there may be a residuum in the prophecy which is world-wide in its bearing. In every such case we fly to the context and to the passages which most nearly resemble the one before us. Sometimes poetical parallelism helps us. Where earth is used in distinction from heaven we take it in the wider sense; where it is distinguished from the Gentile world we take it in the narrower. Sometimes we interpret it of the then known world, as in Gen. **6—9**; whilst the covenant with Noah made in these chapters calls for the use of the word in the widest sense. Neither the Authorised nor the Revised Version has noted the fact that in Gen. **12. 1** the word translated "land" means "earth," whilst in the 3rd verse the word translated "earth" means "land." In later passages where the English is the same, the Hebrew is not so.* The difficulty recurs in some prophetic passages in the New Testament. *[margin: Earth and world.]*

2. We pass from earth to EARTHQUAKES; see, *e.g.* Isai. **13**. 13, and **24**. 19. Are these commotions local? physical? political? The history of the past helps us to some extent. There were literal earthquakes at the giving of the Law and at the crucifixion and resurrection of Christ. We can well understand that physical convulsions may be timed to *[margin: Earthquakes.]*

---

* See *Old Testament Synonyms*, chap. xxiii., on the different Hebrew terms.

take place alongside of national and spiritual upheavals. A combined interpretation thus seems reasonable, though it cannot be pressed. The passages concerning earthquakes in Hag. **2.** 6, 21 are interpreted literally in Heb. **12.** 26–28; and the earthquake of Zech. **14.** 4, etc., is given in such detail that one can hardly regard it as figurative.

Sea and river.

3. THE SEA sometimes stands for a multitude of people, as when Jeremiah (**51.** 42) says, "The sea is come up upon Babylon." The RIVER is used in a similar sense. Thus Isaiah (**8.** 7) says, "Behold, the Lord bringeth up upon them the waters of the river, even the king of Assyria." It does not follow, however, that the sea and the river are never to be taken literally. We read of the coming King, "His dominion shall be from sea to sea, and from the River to the ends of the earth (*i.e.* land)." These words occur both in Ps. **72.** 8 and in Zech. **9.** 10, and refer to the literal boundaries of the Promised Land. The two seas being the Dead Sea and the Mediterranean, the River being the Euphrates, and the ends of the land being the south-west border of Palestine (comp. 1 Kings **4.** 21). The words, "There was no more sea" (Rev. **21.** 1), are capable of both a literal and spiritual interpretation.

Sand.

4. THE SAND of the Sea is frequently referred to as a standard of measurement, as in Gen. **22.** 17 and Hos. **1.** 10; it is not absolute, but stands for a very large number. Thus it is used of the population of Israel in 1 Kings **4.** 20, and of the Midianite camels in Judg. **7.** 12.

Stars.

5. THE STARS OF HEAVEN are referred to in the same way, both in promise (Gen. **15.** 5; **22.** 17), and in history (Deut. **1.** 10). See Heb. **11.** 12.

Darkness.

6. THE DARKENING OF THE SUN, and consequently of its reflector the MOON, and the falling of the STARS (whether planets or meteors) are referred to several times in Scripture,

e.g. Isai. **13**. 10 ; **34**. 4 ; Joel **2**. 10, 31 ; **3**. 15 ; Ezek. **32**. 7 ; Matt. **24**. 29 ; Rev. **6**. 12. In some of these cases there may be a real darkness, as there was at the time when our Lord died ; but in others the words may represent national or world-wide catastrophes, as when we read of dimness and darkness in connexion with captivity (Isai. **8**. 22).

On the other hand, extra brightness and brilliant atmo- *Light.* spheric effects indicate a good time, as when we read, "The light of the moon shall be as the light of the sun, and the light of the sun shall be sevenfold, as the light of seven days" (Isai. **30**. 26). In Isai. **60**. 19, 20 we have what would present an utter inconsistency if the words were translated literally—first, "The sun shall be no more thy light by day, neither for brightness shall the moon give light unto thee"; secondly, "Thy sun shall no more go down, neither shall thy moon withdraw itself"; but in each case there are words added which unify the sense—"The Lord shall be thine everlasting light"; and the two similar passages in the Revelation (**21**. 23; **22**. 5) enforce the great truth that when God is our spiritual light, the need of physical light is only a secondary matter.

The destruction of the earth alone would be a very little thing in the universe; but any catastrophe befalling the sun would ruin our planetary system. Life would cease on earth long before the sun became a dark ball. The diminution of the sun's heat, which some astronomers tell us is already going on or to be expected, would speedily enlarge the glacial zone, and all earth's contents would be frozen up. Even an eclipse of the sun, a sirocco, or a period of darkness in which "Neither sun nor stars appeared in many days" (Acts **27**. 20) would fill the mind with gloom.

7. FIRE is a frequent image; but of what? God Himself *Fire.* is called a consuming fire (Deut. **9**. 3; Heb. **12**. 29). When

He lets the fire of His anger burn up the ungodly, none shall quench it, *i.e.* none shall stay His hand until His purpose is accomplished (Isai. **1.** 31 ; **66.** 24 ; Jer. **4.** 4 ; Mal. **4.** 1 ; Matt. **3.** 12). In Mal. **3.** 2 the fire is purgative rather than retributive and may refer to the testing of men's faith by the fire of persecution and affliction (1 Pet. **1.** 7). The baptism with fire indicates the special energy of the Holy Ghost, who produces spiritual warmth and ardour in the soul. In 2 Pet. **3.** 7, 12 literal fire is apparently predicted, and some such process as that which caused the so-called igneous rocks to be formed may be referred to.

The North. 8. THE NORTH in Biblical times pointed in a somewhat north-easterly direction. It sometimes stands for Assyria (Zeph. **2.** 13), sometimes for Babylon (Jer. **46.** 10), sometimes for the Medo-Persian Empire (Jer. **50.** 9). In Dan. **11.** 6–40 the King of the North seems to be Syria or the Power which holds Syria, and the King of the South is Egypt or the Power which holds Egypt. In Ezek. **26.** 7 Nebuchadnezzar the king of kings is brought from the North ; but in chap. **32.** 30 the Zidonians are called Princes of the North ; and in **38.** 6, 15 the people of Togarmah, *i.e.* the Turcomans, are described, being associated with Gomer, *i.e.* the Cimmerians, and with Gog, Rosh, Meshech, and Tubal, *i.e.* with the Powers now represented by Russia. The fact that the peoples and events mentioned in chaps. **38** and **39** reappear at the close of the Revelation (**19.** 17, 18 ; **20.** 8) invests them with peculiar interest.

Marriage. 9. BETROTHAL and MARRIAGE stand for unity and covenant alliance, whilst DIVORCE marks spiritual separation in consequence of unfaithfulness, which is frequently described as whoredom and adultery. The time of restitution is regarded as re-betrothal. See Hosea, chaps. **1** and **2**. Illustrations from marriage are frequent in all parts of the Bible,

PROPHETIC FORMS OF THOUGHT.

and the "Marriage of the Lamb" appears in the closing scenes of Revelation (chaps. **19.** 7–9 ; **21.** 2, 9). It is difficult to spell out the meaning of these joyful passages ; but the union betwixt Christ and His true Church, which Christians have been aiming at and feeling after for many centuries, will then be accomplished ; and its accomplishment will have a far-reaching influence.

The foregoing nine words are samples of what may be called prophetic forms of thought. We have constantly to remind ourselves that sacred truth can only come to us through the medium of human faculties, and largely through human terminology. Experience gives wider and deeper force to language. When we leave our present life we shall leave many things behind us, and perhaps amongst them our language, together with all the troublesome results of the confusion of tongues. In the spirit-world modes of communication may be utterly different from those with which we are now familiar. Meanwhile we study the Biblical words as so many lights and illustrations, pointing to something better, though in themselves inadequate to convey the whole truth.

CHAPTER VIII.

RECURRENT PROPHETIC FORMULÆ.

THERE are numerous expressions traceable through the prophetic Books which become almost the technical language of prediction. Some of them are connected with our highest hopes as Christians. The following are the most noteworthy :—

1. "*Ye shall know that I am the Lord.*"—This expression springs out of the Book of Exodus (**6. 7**; **16. 12**). It reappears in 1 Kings **20.** 28, and again in Joel (**3. 17**), and is a favourite expression with Ezekiel. It implies a fresh and deeper knowledge of the truth about the Lord Jehovah. The meaning of His Name is only gradually being unfolded in the course of ages. Our convictions are reconstructed and re-interpreted in the light of advancing experience. So it will ever be. There can be no finality in our knowledge of the infinite God, though there may be a great advance (1 Cor. **13.** 12).

2. "*In the last days.*"—A day is a period and may be of any length—a year, a generation, a thousand years. The last days are the latter or later days* as compared with the present, and we must not restrict them to one fixed period. Jacob's blessing on his sons (Gen. **49.** 1) had to do with a time which is now long past, and Balaam's utterance (Num. **24.** 14) must have been shortly fulfilled. The time referred to may be very far off, as in Deut. **4.** 30, which refers to a return after a dispersion (comp. chap. **31.** 29). When

---

* Some students have drawn a distinction between "latter" days and "last" days; but this is hardly justified by the Hebrew or Greek expressions.

we reach the Books of the Prophets the expression seems to point to a more definite period, viz. the time of Restitution, as in Isai. **2.** 2 ; Mic. **4.** 1 ; Hos. **3.** 5. In Jer. **48.** 47 the expression refers to Moab, the prophecy of Balaam being taken up, but it gives a hope for Moab which Balaam's words did not offer. Compare the case of Elam (Jer. **49.** 39). In Dan. **10.** 14 the fulfilment extends through a long period, and in the case of Ezek. **38.** 8, 16 it may be yet in the future. The expression recurs in the New Testament. See especially 2 Tim. **3.** 1 ; Jas. **5.** 3 ; 2 Pet. **3.** 3, all of which apparently refer to the future. The expression "the last day," used by the Lord in John **6.** 39, 40, 44, 54, manifestly refers to the period of Resurrection, which may synchronise with the Restitution.

3. "*The day of the Lord.*"—This is the time of the manifestation of some special attribute or purpose of God. In Isai. **2.** 12 it marks a judicial crisis ; in Ezek. **13.** 5 a day of battle ; in Amos **5.** 18 it is pointed out that the day will prove very different from what some people expected. In the New Testament it refers to a time then (if not now) future—a bright and happy day, a time of salvation and of manifestation. See especially 1 Cor. **1.** 8 ; **5.** 5 ; 2 Cor. **1.** 14.

4. "*The day of the Lord is at hand.*"—The R.V. substitutes "near" for "at hand." This expression had to do with the fall of Babylon (Isai. **13.** 6), with the punishment of Egypt (Ezek. **30.** 3), and with the destruction of Israel and Jerusalem (Joel **1.** 15 ; Zeph. **1.** 7, 14, 18). Similar expressions which refer to temporal judgments may be noted in Isai. **13.** 9 ; Joel **2.** 1 ; and Zech. **14.** 1. These passages throw light on kindred utterances in the New Testament, and justify us in looking upon the fall of Jerusalem (A.D. 70) as a special manifestation of the day of the Lord ; though the full force of the expression is yet in the future.

5. "*The Lord cometh.*"—The expression may be as old as Enoch (Jude 14). It refers to various visitations and actions of God, Who is always regarded in Scripture as the Judge of all the earth. He comes to punish (Isai. **26**. 21), to save (Isai. **40**. 10), to visit His temple (Mal. **3**. 1), and to visit Zion (Isai. **59**. 20). The words imply something providential, but not necessarily a visible apparition. There is often something sudden and startling about it, and there may be external manifestations in connexion with it which exceed all that we can conceive in sublimity and glory. The suddenness is exhibited by the word "quickly" (*i.e.* suddenly); see Rev. **3**. 11; **22**. 7, 20; and the visitations are sometimes compared to a snare, to lightning, or to the inroad of a thief in the night (1 Thess. **5**. 2; 2 Pet. **3**. 10; Rev. **3**. 3; **16**. 15). Those, however, who watch need not be taken unprepared (Luke **12**. 39; **21**. 34; 1 Thess. **5**. 4).

The second coming of Christ is sometimes spoken of as an *Epiphany* or Manifestation, like the first (Heb. **9**. 26, 28); sometimes it is denoted by the word *Parousia* (παρουσία), which means either presence or coming. This word is not found in the LXX. except in the Second Book of Maccabees; but it is used four times in Matt. **24**, and several times in the Epistles of St. Paul, St. James, St. Peter, and St. John, generally in connexion with the Lord's second coming. The attendant circumstances have to be gathered from the context.

There are other expressions allied to those which have been touched upon, *e.g.* the Day of the Lord's Vengeance, the Day of Judgment, the Day of Visitation, and the Last Day. Also most of the prophets use the expression "In that day." An examination of the passages where this phrase occurs will incline us to the belief that it stands for a period rather than for a point of time, as is the case with similar expressions. In some passages the time referred to is already past; in others it appears to be still future. Isaiah is particularly fond of speaking of "that day," as in chap. **19**, which refers to Egypt, and chap. **24.** 21, which refers to the Restitution. In Matt. **7.** 22 our Lord uses the words with reference to the future, when the destiny of all men shall be decided.

6. "*The turning of the Captivity*" is first referred to in Deuteronomy. The going into captivity in consequence of wrong doing had already been predicted (chap. **28.** 41). The subsequent turning of the Captivity, *i.e.* liberation and restoration, is promised to those who turn to the Lord with all their heart (**30.** 3). The thought is reproduced in Hos. **6.** 11; Joel **3.** 1; and Amos **9.** 14. It frequently occurs in the Psalms (**14.** 7; **53.** 6; **85.** 1; **126.** 1, 4), and is taken up again by the Captivity prophets—Jeremiah and Ezekiel, *e.g.* Jer. **30.** 3 and Ezek. **39.** 25. The passages referred to were partly fulfilled in the restoration under Zerubbabel, but the prospect held out in some of them was never fully realised. The expression is also used of the restoration of foreign nations, *e.g.* Moab and Ammon and Egypt (Jer. **48.** 47; **49.** 6; Ezek. **29.** 14).

There is no difference in Hebrew between turning, returning, conversion, and being restored. Sometimes the word "return" is used in conjunction with another word in the sense of "again." Thus, in Hos. **3.** 5, we read, "Afterwards shall the children of Israel return and seek the Lord." This does not mean that they shall first return to their land and then seek the Lord, but simply that they will seek the Lord again. So in Dan. **9.** 25, the words "to restore and to build Jerusalem" mean "to re-build Jerusalem."

The Return or Restitution in a national and territorial sense is perhaps best illustrated from Lev. **25.** 10. In the year of Jubilee every one returned to his possession and to his family. It was a time of liberty (*v*. 10), such as is pictured up in Isai. **61**. 1, 2, which the Lord Jesus claimed as being fulfilled in His day. The trumpet sounded through the land (Isai. **27**. 13) to announce the acceptable year of the Lord. The Restitution passages are numerous in Isaiah, Hosea, Jeremiah, and other prophets. Their fulfilment is not yet completed. The Apostles asked our Lord about it on the day of His ascension. Probably they expected it at once (Acts **1**. 6); at any rate, they saw shortly afterwards that Restitution in its full sense could not be accomplished till the Lord's return. The heavens must receive Him (*i.e.* must retain Him) until the times of the Restitution of all the things whereof God spake by the mouth of His holy prophets from old time* (Acts **3**. 21).

7. "*The remnant shall return.*"—This is the meaning of the Hebrew name Shear Jashub (Isai. **7**. 3). The word *shear* signifies "what is left," like the gleaning of grapes. It is translated "posterity" in Gen. **45**. 7, where the R.V. has rightly put "remnant." In this passage and in later utterances a second word is associated with it (פליתה), which signifies "those that escape." The words are used under varying circumstances, being applied not only to Israel, but to Syria, Ashdod, Ammon, etc. In the age of Hezekiah and Manasseh Israel was already regarded as a remnant (2 Kings **19**. 4; **21**. 14); but though a remnant, they were cared for by God, and though they must needs go into captivity, yet there should always be a *residuum* of the Tribes in whom God would fulfil His ancient promises. So we read (Isai. **10**. 21, 22), "The remnant shall return, even the remnant of Jacob unto the mighty God. For though thy people Israel

---

* Why the Revisers retained the strange English exaggeration "since the world began" it is hard to conceive.

be as the sand of the sea (yet only) a remnant of them shall return." We can trace the promises to the remnant through Isaiah, Joel, Amos, Micah, Zephaniah, and onward through Jeremiah and Ezekiel to the days of Zechariah and of Nehemiah (**11. 20**). In Rom. **9. 27** and **11. 5** the idea is taken up. There is still a remnant according to the election of grace.

It is curious to trace the numerical proportion of the remnant to the main body of Israel. When the spies went to Canaan two were faithful and ten unfaithful. In Elijah's time 7,000 of the people of the Northern Kingdom were loyal to God. In Isai. **6. 13** the remnant to return is a tenth (comp. Amos **5. 3**). In Ezek. **5** the people are divided into three thirds: one dies of pestilence and famine; one falls by the sword; one is scattered and slain; but a very small number are preserved, their preservation being symbolised by a few hairs from the prophet's head being bound up in his flowing sleeves.

8. "*All nations*."—It is a question sometimes what amount of universality is to be given to this expression. In Gen. **10. 32**, we read, "These are the families of the sons of Noah, after their generations, in their nations, and by these were the nations divided in the earth after the flood." This passage seems to be referred to in Deut. **32. 8**: "When the most High divided to the nations their inheritance, when He separated the sons of Adam, He set the bounds of the peoples according to the number of the children of Israel." In other words, the arrangement of the nationalities was determined with a view to the special requirements of Israel (comp. Acts **17. 26**). In Gen. **12. 3** "all the families of the land" are to receive a blessing in Abraham. In chap. **18. 18** they are described as "all the nations of the earth;" comp. **22. 18**. The promise reappears in Acts **3. 25**. It can hardly be narrowed

down to the tribes of Canaan or the neighbouring nations. It looks world-wide. Sometimes, however, the expression is limited in the context, as in Deut. **30.** 1, 3, where the nations are those among whom Israel was to be scattered. The same may be said of Luke **21.** 24, which declares that Israel should be led away captive into all nations. The promise, "I will set thee on high above all nations of the earth" (Deut. **28.** 1), looks unlimited as to space, though it might be restricted as to time. It is difficult to put restrictions on a number of passages in the Psalms and Prophets, *e.g.* Ps. **22.** 27, "All the ends of the world shall remember and turn unto the Lord, and all the kindreds of the nations shall worship before thee"; comp. Ps. **72.** 11, 17, and **86.** 9. See also Isai. **2.** 2, "all nations shall flow unto it." In Isai. **66.** 18, 20 the words seem to be in a more restricted sense. In Dan. **7.** 14 we are told that "all peoples, nations, and languages" shall serve the Son of Man. Here the expression looks unlimited; but the very same words are used in chap. **6.** 25 of the population of the Medo-Persian Empire. A similar limitation is implied in Acts **2.** 5. But what are we to say of Joel **3.** 2, 12, and of the somewhat corresponding passage, Matt. **25.** 32? In Matt. **24.** 14 the Lord Jesus says that "the Gospel of the kingdom is to be preached in all the world for a witness to all nations." This is surely world-wide, and helps us to solve more obscure passages. Sometimes the expression may stand for all the nations who happen to be existing at some particular crisis; and this is the view held by some in connexion with the so-called parable of the sheep and the goats (Matt. **25**).

The expression "many nations" occurs in some passages in a world-wide sense, *e.g.* Isai. **52.** 15, "he shall sprinkle many nations"; comp. Zech. **2.** 11, "many nations shall be joined to the Lord in that day." In Gen. **17.** 4 we are told that Abraham's family was to become "many nations," or as it is in chap. **28**. 3, "an assemblage of peoples" (comp. **48**. 4). Each tribe practically became a "nation" in the sense in which the Perizzites, Hivites, and Jebusites were nations.

9. "*The Tabernacle of God is with men.*"—When Moses received instructions to make a Tent or Tabernacle it was to be a place of meeting between God and man. In Exod. **29**. 42 God says of the Tabernacle of the congregation, there "I will meet you to speak unto thee," the same root supplying the words used for "congregation" and "meet." Hence the Revisers have rightly substituted "meeting" for "congregation"; but we have to remember that the word means *a meeting by appointment.** The passage proceeds (*v.* 45), "and I will dwell among the children of Israel and be their God." The word here translated "dwell" is the origin of the word *Shekinah*, which simply means dwelling-place, and is specially associated with the idea of a tent. The word has found its way into Greek and other languages, and is used in John **1**. 14, where we are told of the *Logos* that He pitched His tent among us. When the Temple was dedicated Solomon felt that God could not really be contained within the compass of a Temple built with hands (1 Kings **8**. 27); but God promised, "I will dwell among the children of Israel" (1 Kings **6**. 13). The thought recurs in Ezek. **37**. 27, 28, "My tabernacle shall be with them—My sanctuary shall be in the midst of them for evermore." Later on we find the same truth in Zech. **2**. 10, 11, "I will dwell in the midst of thee," and chap. **8**. 3, "I will dwell in the midst of Jerusalem"; and the Book of Revelation closes with the accomplishment of this significant promise (Rev. **21**. 3), "Behold, the Tabernacle of God is with men and He will dwell with them."

---

* See *Old Testament Synonyms,* chap. 19.

In many of these passages another promise runs alongside of the first, viz.: "*I will be their God and they shall be My people.*" We find the two in juxtaposition in Lev. **26**. 11, 12, also in Jeremiah and Ezekiel and elsewhere. When Israel was chosen to be a people of God, it was as a sample nation (Exod. **19.** 5); but the promise was not absolutely restricted to them. St. Paul takes Ezekiel's words and applies them freely to the Corinthians (comp. Ezek. **37**. 26, 27, with 2 Cor. **6**. 16, etc.), and so it is in the passage quoted from the Book of Revelation, above. The Divine intention towards man can never be completely realised until the union between God and a considerable selection, if not the vast mass, of human beings is an accomplished fact.

10. "*The end of the world.*"—The English word "end" stands for various Hebrew words. It sometimes means a purpose, sometimes a closing period, sometimes a final act. In Gen. **6**. 13 we read "The end of all flesh is come before Me." It was as if the life of man upon earth were about to close, as if human beings were to become an extinct species. In Num. **23.** 10 Balaam expresses the wish that his "last end" may be like that of the upright. Probably the "final condition"—the condition after death—is here referred to. In Ezek. **7**. 2 the prophet says concerning the land of Israel, "An end, the end is come upon the four corners of the land; now is the end upon thee." This was not an absolute end, but a temporary close of national prosperity and a time of judgment and retribution. This is the key to the whole of this striking chapter.

Turning to the New Testament we find the same variety of meaning in the use of the word "end." Our Lord draws certain distinctions in Matt. **24** when replying to the questions of His disciples. After speaking of wars He says (*v.* 6), "The end is not yet;" but when the Gospel has been preached to all nations, "Then shall the end come." In 1 Cor. **15**. 24, when St. Paul says "Then cometh the end," he refers to the putting down of all enemies under Christ's feet, of which the closing act is the resurrection of the dead. It is clear that "the end" spoken of in such passages may be national or world-wide. It has to do with what we ordinarily call a dispensation. There was an Israelite dispensation which closed with the fall of Jerusalem. There is a Gentile dispensation now running on. There is another dispensation in which Gentiles and Jews will rejoice together. What shall the spiritual restoration of Israel be in that day but "life from the dead" (Rom. **11**. 15). This may be the period spoken of in Dan. **12**. 13 : "Go thou thy way till the end ; for thou shalt rest, and thou shalt stand in thy lot at the end of the days."

In the New Testament it is noteworthy that the expression "*the end of the world*" is only found in St. Matthew (**13**. 39, 40, 49 ; **24**. 3 ; **28**. 20). It signifies the consummation or completion of the age. It is a great time of decision and discrimination. The expression in Heb. **9**. 26 is slightly different, the word for "world" being in the plural.

11. "*The Kingdom of God.*"—The idea of God as king comes to the front in Exod. **15**. 18, and again in 1 Sam. **12**. 12. The appointment of an earthly king called for the assertion of the Royal position of the true King of kings. The Psalms abound with references to it, and it is the underlying thought in many of the prophets (see, *e.g.* Isai. **6**. 5). The Lord was to reign in Mount Zion and in Jerusalem before His elders gloriously (Isai. **24**. 23 ; Mic. **4**. 7 ; Obad. 21). The fulfilment of this passage is dated by Micah as "in the latter days," when the Remnant would become a strong nation. It was evidently to be something definite and demonstrable ; something far different from what has ever been seen in Jewish history. In the 7th of Daniel the Kingdom of God

thus anticipated is more fully described. The kingdom is given to the Son of Man (*v.* 14) and to the saints (*vv.* 18, 27). The period of this kingdom is marked to some extent by being associated with the final break up of the sub-divided Fourth Empire, and the downfall of a special power which should spring up from the ashes of that empire. It thus stands over unfulfilled as yet.

On turning to the New Testament we are confronted with the appearance of this kingdom as "at hand," and yet when St. Paul's Epistles were written, and when the Book of the Revelation was written, it was in prospect at some time not clearly revealed. The king had come, and seeds of the kingdom had been sown, subjects were being accumulated; but the coming of the Son of Man in His Kingdom, so graphically described in St. Matthew, was still in the future. Even when we strip the passages concerning the kingdom of all that is earthly, national, and political, it is clear that we must look ahead for the fulfilment of the promise.

12. *The glory of God.*—In Exod. **16**. 6, 7 we read, "At even, then ye shall know that it is the Lord who hath brought you out from the land of Egypt; and in the morning, then ye shall see the glory of God." There was to be a practical demonstration of God which should appeal to their senses. The fulfilment of the promise was realised in the gift of bread from heaven. In chap. **24**. 16, 17, "the glory of the Lord" was like a consuming fire on the top of the mount. This was an appeal to the eye, and the grandeur of the sight would impress the mind with a sense of awe. The time of Restitution is associated with the glory of the Lord in Isai. **35**. 2 : "They shall see the glory of the Lord and the excellency of our God." So in chap. **40**. 5 : "The glory of the Lord shall be unveiled, and all flesh shall see it together." There was evidently to be a great manifestation of the Divine excellencies

at a time then future. In John **1.** 14 this manifestation is said to have been effected in Christ, the only-begotten Son. It was specially exhibited, however, not so much in startling effects as in free grace and in truth. Even the Apostles desired a further demonstration of God, but they were taught to see in Him, as their Master, all that heart and conscience could desire (John **14.** 9–12). As the recall of Lazarus was a special mark of God's glory (John **11.** 40), so the resurrection and ascension of Christ, together with the outpouring of the Spirit, constituted a proof that God had glorified His Son (Acts **3.** 13). The return of Christ "without sin unto salvation" will be the crowning demonstration of the majesty, power, and goodness of God.

CHAPTER IX.

THE FUTURE EXPRESSED IN TERMS OF THE PAST. NOTE ON "THE SON OF DAVID."

IN examining the forms of prophetic thought in Scripture we find none so common as the expression of the future in terms borrowed from the historic past. This is done either formally, by direct comparison, or indirectly by allusion or mystical identification.

Past events utilised.

i. The following are the most notable illustrations of events narrated in the Pentateuch, and utilised by the prophets for predictive purposes :—

1. *Creation.*—The fact that God created the heavens and the earth is laid down as a fundamental truth in Scripture, though no attempt is made to explain the process. In Isai. **65.** 17 and **66.** 22 the promise of a new creation of heaven and earth is laid down with equal clearness. St. Peter appeals to this promise (2 Pet. **3.** 13), giving further details; and in Rev. **21.** 1 the work of re-creation is regarded as accomplished. As the first creation was practically such a renovation of the earth's surface as made it habitable for man (Ps. **104.** 30), so the new creation may be a fresh adaptation of earth for the requirements of the risen race.

2. *Paradise.*—In Gen. **2.** 8 we find man placed in the Garden of Eden or Paradise. The Tree of Life is in the midst, and the Water of Life flows thence into the outer world. In Isai. **51.** 3 we have a direct comparison : "The Lord will comfort Zion : He will comfort all her waste places : He will make her wilderness like Eden, and her desert like

the Garden of the Lord" (comp. Zech. **1**. 17, where the first part of this utterance is taken up). In Rev. **2**. 7 we have a mystical identification of the Tree of Life with the source of spiritual sustenance in the world to come. "To him that overcometh will I give to eat of the Tree of Life which is in the midst of the Paradise of God." See also chap. **22**. 1, 2.

3. *The Deluge.*—The reference to the waters of Noah in Isai. **54**. 9 is a direct comparison. In 2 Pet. **3**. 5 it is the same; but instead of "water," the destroying agent is "fire." Comp. chap. **2**. 5.

4. *The destruction of Sodom and Gomorrah.*—This is taken as a type or sample of God's dealing with the ungodly. See Deut. **29**. 23; compare 2 Pet. **2**. 6. In Isai. **1**. 9, 10 Israel's fate is first compared with that of Sodom and Gomorrah, and then the people are called by the names of these cities, as rulers of Sodom and people of Gomorrah. In Rev. **11**. 8 the dead bodies of the two witnesses are "in the street of the great city which is spiritually (*i.e.* mystically) called Sodom and Egypt, where also the Lord was crucified." Comp. Jer. **23**. 14, "They are all unto Me as Sodom, and the inhabitants thereof as Gomorrah." The nature of the sin of Sodom is described in Ezek. **16**. 49; and in the 53rd verse (strange as it may seem) a hope is held out even for the restoration of these evil cities. Compare Matt. **10**. 15 and **11**. 24—passages in which our Lord throws a hopeful light on the condition of those who had died in their sin under the older dispensation.

The passages concerning the lake of fire and brimstone (Rev. **19**. 20, etc.) are expressed in language borrowed from the physical fate of the cities of the Plain (Gen. **19**. 24). Comp. Ps. **11**. 6 and Ezek. **38**. 22. The going up of the smoke (Rev. **14**. 11, etc.) may be attributed to the same scene, as it is described in Gen. **19**. 28 ; it is also spoken of in Jude 7 as "eternal fire." In such cases the terms must not be pressed too literally. It seems best to dwell on the moral and spiritual aspects of the case, without, however, forgetting that as there is a physical side to sin, so there is appointed a physical side to retribution.

5. *Egyptian bondage.*—In Deut. **28**, after warning Israel that the plagues of Egypt would be visited upon the people in case of their disobedience (*vv.* 27, 60), Moses says, "The Lord shall bring thee into Egypt again with ships, by the way whereof I spake unto thee (saying), Thou shalt see it no more again, and there ye shall be sold unto your enemies for bondmen and bondwomen, and no man shall buy you." Taken literally these words seem a collection of paradoxes; but confining our attention to the first part of the utterance, it is important to notice that Hosea takes up the thought. He says, in chap. **8**. 13, "They shall return to Egypt"; chap. **9**. 3, "Ephraim shall return to Egypt"; verse 6, "Egypt shall gather them up . . . . Memphis shall bury them." But in chap. **11**. 5 the literal interpretation receives a direct negative—"He shall not return into the land of Egypt, but the Assyrian shall be his king." (Comp. Jer. **16**. 14, 15.)

We saw above (§ 4) that Jerusalem was spiritually or mystically called both Sodom and Egypt. Why the latter ? Not because Israel was an oppressor, but because the people were liable to the plagues of Egypt in consequence of their sin. See Amos **4**. 10, 11, where Egypt and Sodom are named together in this sense: "I have sent among you the pestilence after the manner of Egypt . . . . I have overthrown some of you as God overthrew Sodom." The reappearance of the Egyptian plagues in the Apocalypse is noteworthy.

6. *The Exodus.*—The crossing of the Red Sea dryshod is referred to in Isaiah, who foretells the destruction of the

tongue of the Egyptian sea, so that men may go over dry-shod (Isai. 11. 15). The passage, however, is not to be taken literally, for the next verse says that it is the return of the remnant from Assyria (not from Egypt) which is thus described. The song of praise which follows is based on Miriam's Song (comp. Isai. 12. 2 with Exod. 15. 2). So says Hosea (2. 15), "She shall sing . . . . as in the day when she came up out of the land of Egypt." In Isai. 27. 12, 13 the Exodus from Egypt seems again to furnish materials for describing the return from Assyria. Compare Zech. 10. 10, 11, which takes up the language of Isaiah and Hosea concerning Assyria and Egypt, though really other nations must be here referred to as the oppressors of Israel.

7. *Wilderness life.*—The pillar of fire and cloud (the same pillar being luminous by night, but non-luminous by day) presents a picture of Divine overshadowing presence in Isai. 4. 5. Streams in the desert furnish part of the graphic description of Israel's redeemed life in Isai. 35; comp. chap. 43. The giving of the Law at Sinai becomes suitable clothing for the appeal of Isai. 64; and the valley of Achor is once more to be a door of hope, according to Hos. 2. 15.

It is remarkable that it is mainly to the Pentateuch that the prophets look for illustrations of the future; though there are occasional comparisons with events in the days of the Judges and Kings. See Hos. 9. 9; 10. 9; and Isai. 28. 21, compared with 2 Sam. 5. 20, 25.

ii. As future events are clothed in language borrowed from the past, so it is with persons, some of whom occupied a specially representative position in ancient times. *Names of persons utilised.*

1. The first case to consider is that of ELIJAH. This prophet had produced a profound impression on his own times. Some four centuries after his rapture, the Prophet

Malachi utters these words, "Behold, I will send you Elijah the prophet before the coming of the great and terrible day of the Lord." But was he literally to return? If not, in what sense is the passage to be understood? The scribes in our Lord's time seem to have taken the words literally; and the Jews still put a place for him at the Paschal supper, and open the door for him. When John the Baptist was to be born, the Angel Gabriel said that he was to act in the spirit and power of Elijah (in some such sense as Elisha did), and so to be his representative and carry on his work. Accordingly, when John was asked if he was Elijah he answered, No; and yet the Lord Jesus claimed John as the promised Elijah (Matt. **11. 14**). With regard to the time of the predicted appearance, it was to be before "the coming of the great and terrible day of the Lord." This expression takes us back to Joel **2. 31**, where it is associated with the outpouring of the Spirit; and this association is supported by John himself, whose baptism was to lead up to the baptism with the Holy Ghost. But the words of Mal. **4. 5** cannot be read apart from those of Mal. **3. 1**; and these are claimed as fulfilled in John—"Behold, I will send My messenger, and he shall prepare the way before Me." This utterance again takes us back to Isai. **40. 3**, "The voice of one crying in the wilderness, Prepare ye the way of the Lord." We thus possess a chain of thought, exhibited in Isaiah, reproduced with further definiteness in Malachi, and embodied in the mission of John. Perhaps there is yet an unfulfilled *residuum* in the prediction.

2. There is thus clearly established the idea of the appearance of a representative man whose mission was reproduced in later ages by one who is mystically identified with him. This leads us to look with favour on the thought that others may be in some degree representative. There

THE FUTURE EXPRESSED IN TERMS OF THE PAST. 71

are two men who were actually named long before they were born, JOSIAH and CYRUS, one a reformer and the other a deliverer, and each may be taken in some degree as representing far greater work than they actually did in their own persons. JONAH was representative also. His wonderful deliverance seems to give form to Hosea's utterance, "After two days He will revive us; in the third day He will raise us up" (Hos. 6. 2). He became a representative afterwards in the matter of preaching repentance, and the Lord Jesus takes the strange and unheard of event which befell him as something to be realised in His own case. ELIAKIM (Isai. 22. 15-25) was also in this sense representative or typical. The key of the house of David which was put upon his shoulder as a sign of government reminds us of a greater Governor (Isai. 9. 6), and the position is claimed for Christ, together with the words that follow, in Rev. 3. 7.

JESHUA and ZERUBBABEL are also typical. The one is the Prince of David's line, and the other the high priest. Both are deliverers and Temple-builders, and so types of Christ (Hag. 2; Zech. 3, 4, 6).

3. Lastly we come to DAVID, whose case demands more careful consideration. There is a promise made to David which is of a very definite character. It is to be found in 2 Sam. 7 and 1 Chron. 17, and in a poetical form in Ps. 89. It is referred to more than once in the Historical Books, and in various Psalms, *e.g.* Ps. 132. Sometimes the promise in question is spoken of as destined to be realised in the Seed, the Branch, which God would raise up, or cause to grow up, out of the root of Jesse. Sometimes David himself is spoken of. Belonging to the first class are such passages as Isai. 9. 7, where the Prince is described as sitting on David's throne; see also Isai. 11. 10, when the root of

The case of David.

Jesse is to be sought after by the Gentiles. Comp. chaps. **16.** 5; **55.** 3; Amos **9.** 11; Jer. **23.** 5; Zech. **12.** 7–10.

The other class of passages will include Hos. **3.** 5, "Afterward shall the children of Israel return and seek the Lord their God and David their king"; Jer. **30.** 9, "They shall serve the Lord and David their king whom I will raise up to them"; Ezek. **34.** 23, 24, "They shall have one shepherd . . . . My servant David"; chap. **37.** 22–25, "One king shall be king to them all . . . . and David My servant shall be king over them . . . . and My servant David shall be their prince for ever."

Interpreting the second class of passages in the light of the first, we see that the promised king in these passages is really not the literal, but the ideal David, the mystical head of a re-united people with whom the Gentiles should be associated. He is one of the House of David, and claims the name of Son of David; and certain promises made to David are fulfilled in Him.

Turning to the New Testament we have the record of One whose genealogy is traced back to David, who is frequently claimed as Son of David; in whom are fulfilled passages ascribed to David, *e.g.* Pss. **2, 16, 22, 89, 110, 118**, and other passages referred to above. Of Him we read, "He shall be great, and shall be called the Son of the Most High; and the Lord shall give unto Him the throne of His father David; and He shall reign over the house of Jacob for ever; and of His kingdom there shall be no end" (Luke **1.** 32, 33). Later on these words are put into His mouth, "I am the root and the offspring of David" (Rev. **22.** 16).

We thus get a chain of promise and fulfilment covering a period of a thousand years, and unfolding the prospect of an ideal and permanent Davidic kingdom. It may be asked what there was in David which should make him such a conspicuous figure. The answer seems to be that in certain points of character, position, and action, He who should come would fulfil and realise and (may we say?) idealise what we see presented in rude outline in the literal David. Students may draw out these points differently; but it is clear that the man who was in some respects after God's heart, and who should in some slight degree do all God's will (Acts **13**. 22), is thrown altogether into the shade by another who was absolutely after God's own heart, and who came into the world to do all God's will.

iii. Before passing on to the next chapter it ought to be pointed out that not only individuals, but nations, were largely representative. Dr. Arnold's view of prophecy was that it is the inspired utterance of God's purpose that good shall triumph over evil. Certain nations, he thought, represented certain principles or characteristics, and we can read the history and destiny of modern nations in their light. Thus Babylon might represent worldliness, Egypt pride, Edom the unbrotherly brother, Tyre and Zidon commercial enterprise. This view certainly deserves consideration, though it hardly satisfies all the requirements of the prophetic passages.

Representative nations

Note.—In what sense is it true that Jesus was the Son of David?

1. The genealogies contained in Matt. **1** and Luke **3** sufficiently establish, and on independent grounds, that Joseph was the lineal descendant of David; and they make it probable, if not certain, that if the throne of David were to be re-established Joseph would be the person on whose head the crown would be placed. Accordingly he is called the Son of David both in Matt. **1**. 20 and in Luke **1**. 27.

2. It is equally clear from Matt. **1** and Luke **1** that Joseph was not literally the father of Jesus, though Mary was literally His mother. Joseph, however, acted the part of father to him The child was born under Joseph's protection, and grew up under his guardianship; and as Pharaoh's daughter adopted Moses as her son, so Joseph adopted Jesus as his son. He is called in Luke **3.** 23 the reputed father, and in this sense Mary speaks to Jesus, saying, "Thy father and I have sought thee sorrowing;" and the two are called his "parents."

3. To what tribe Mary belonged is not absolutely certain; but her kinship with Elizabeth does not preclude her from being a Judean, intermarriage between the tribes of Judah and Levi being traceable back to the time of Aaron. The words in Luke **1.** 32, "the Lord shall give unto Him the throne of His father David," seem hardly consistent with any other view than that Mary was of the lineage of David, and no difficulty on this score seems to have occurred to her mind. Whether she was summoned to Bethlehem because she was an heiress in her own right, or whether she shrank from separation from Joseph at this critical moment, or whether she received direction from God in the matter, is not told us. All three views may be true.

4. The Evangelists, however, never discuss the genealogy of Mary. They consider it enough to establish the claim of Joseph. Peter and Paul in preaching about Christ say that the Lord Jesus was "raised up" unto David as his seed (Acts **2.** 30; **13.** 22, 23, 33; comp. Luke **1.** 69). In the Epistles He is said to have "sprung" from the tribe of Judah (Heb. **7.** 14), and to be of the seed of David according to the flesh (Rom. **1.** 3), being the Lion of the Tribe of Judah (Rev. **5.** 5), and the root and offspring of David (Rev. **22.** 16).

5. We are thus led to the conclusion that our Lord's

position as Son of David was established, humanly speaking, by the action of Joseph in adopting Him, rather than by the fact that Mary was in all probability of David's descent. Succession in the kingly line was not altogether by birth, but by appointment. Solomon was appointed to succeed David both by Divine direction and by David's own decree. When we read that Jeconiah begat Shealtiel (Matt. **1. 12**) we are not to understand that Shealtiel was literally the son of Jeconiah, but that he was his genealogical successor. So in other cases. If Joseph had been asked on whom among his possible heirs the crown of David should be placed, there seems no doubt as to what his answer would be.

CHAPTER X.

THE PREDICTIVE ELEMENT IN THE SACRIFICIAL SYSTEM.

FROM the earliest times worship has found its expression in ritual. Bodily actions, such as the lifting up of the hands, or the bending of the knees, or the prostration of the whole body, have symbolised spiritual needs and a sense of dependence on the Unseen. In sacrificial feasts and offerings there has always been more or less clearly expressed the thought of what was due to God, and the desire for communion with Him and with one another. Primæval and patriarchal ritual was simple, but it tended to become more complicated, especially when the Mosaic system was ordained. Technical words and ceremonial ordinances were freely introduced; and whilst some parts of the Levitical system were sanitary and social, others had to do with the mode of approach to God on the part of His imperfect and unworthy children. It is noteworthy that Moses gave no instructions about prayer. The people's attention was mainly directed to offerings, almost all of which involved the death of victims. Our business is now to inquire whether these rites were in any sense predictive as well as symbolical.

Pictorial rites and objects.

1. First, it is noteworthy that the whole Levitical system claims to be a revelation; it purports to have been given through Moses, but was not invented by him. This prepares us for the possibility that some at least of the ordinances might be a foreshadowing of a future event which should bridge over the painful and mysterious gulf which exists between man and God.

THE PREDICTIVE ELEMENT IN SACRIFICES. 77

2. Secondly, we are told over and over again that Moses was to make all things according to the patterns or types showed him in vision (Exod. **25.** 9, 40 ; comp. 1 Chron. **28.** 12, 19). He saw heavenly things and was instructed to represent them by earthly objects and rites (Heb. **8.** 4, 5).

A special sacredness thus attached itself to such objects as the altar, the tabernacle, the veil, and the sanctuary; they had been constructed according to type, and were to be regarded as shadows of better things. This accounts for some expressions in the Psalms and Prophets, and prepares the way for the teaching of the Epistle to the Hebrews, and of the New Testament generally. By the light of these books we learn that the House of God points to a spiritual house, built of living stones; the moveable sanctuary teaches that the Lord's Body would be constantly present, yet capable of being taken down and built up again; the veil between the Holy and Most Holy symbolised that the way to God was barred in some degree under the old system; but it is done away in Christ. The Jewish writers Josephus and Philo are fanciful in their interpretations, but both see that there was a hidden meaning in the old ritual.

3. Again, there were certain sacred persons for whom we English happen to have no corresponding word, so that we borrow one from another department and call them priests, *i.e.* presbyters. These *Cohens* or priests were privileged persons who had a special right of access to God. They had various functions, civil and medical, as well as religious; but their most noteworthy function was the sprinkling of the life-blood of certain victims on the altar, a task which in patriarchal days was performed by the head of each family or clan. The choice of the House of Aaron as the priestly house was confirmed in a special way by the great Resurrection type (Num. **3.** 7, 8); and the budding,

Typical offices.

blossoming, and fruit-bearing rod was to be preserved alongside of the tablets of the Law and the jar of manna, with the intention of fixing its meaning on the mind of generations to come, when the Law should be fulfilled in Christ, and He should become the Bread of Life and the High Priest of His people. Meanwhile priesthood is no longer confined to a family. All Christians have the right of access to God in Christ.

Typical offerings.

4. The instructions in Leviticus concerning the offerings and sacrifices are very minute, and abound in technicalities which are usually lost in translation, as in our Authorised and Revised Versions.* Thus, in the first chapter of Leviticus the offering is turned to vapour (not "burnt," in the sense of being "burnt up") and so ascends; this indicates the acceptance of the worshipper, who has identified himself with it and appropriated it by the laying on of hands. The remarkable rites of the Day of Atonement (Lev. **16**) stand in contrast with all others; and the victims represent certain stages of atonement. First, there is death, then liberation, then ascension. The first provides cleansing blood and justifies God in dwelling amongst a sinful people; the second typifies the resurrection—for the escape-goat, according to the ritual, goes off free into the desert, the two goats representing two stages in one event; the third is the burnt-offering, which illustrates the ascension. The meaning of these rites could not be read at the time. They stood as enigmas; but we Christians have not to strain the text unnaturally to see in them the death, resurrection, and ascension of Christ.

The first-fruits.

5. Among periodical rites attention may be called to the first-fruits. In Lev. **23** we read of the handful of first-

---

* See the discussion of the leading technical words here referred to, in *Old Testament Synonyms* (Nisbet).

THE PREDICTIVE ELEMENT IN SACRIFICES. 79

fruits artificially ripened and waved before the Lord on the third day, *i.e.* the morrow after the Paschal Sabbath (comp. **2.** 12, 14). This is what is called "The first of the first-fruits" (Exod. **23.** 19). Fifty days later came the natural first-fruits, on the Day of Pentecost. The periods exactly tally with the time of the resurrection of Christ, Who was the first-fruits in one sense (1 Cor. **15.** 23), and the outpouring of the Spirit on the first believers, who became the first-fruits of the Christian community in another sense (Lev. **23.** 15, 16; Num. **28.** 26).

6. It is not surprising that Levitical and sacrificial language should be used in a spiritual and prophetic sense in the later Books, the worship of the future being expressed in them in a general way without calling for a rigid literal interpretation. Thus, in Isai. **56.** 7 outsiders are regarded as being brought to God's House of Prayer, and their sacrifices as being accepted on His altar (comp. **60.** 7); so Gentiles are to be taken for priests and Levites, and there is to be worship on new moons and Sabbaths (Isai. **66.** 20, 23). Jeremiah's words are very strong in chap. **33.** 18, etc., "The priests the Levites shall not want a man before Me to offer burnt-offerings, meat-offerings, and sacrifices." The covenant made with them shall not be broken, and they shall be innumerable. It is to be observed that the same thing is said of the seed of David in the context, so that the expressions must be interpreted together. Similarly in Ezek. **43.** 19 and **44.** 15, "the priests the Levites of Zadok's seed" are regarded as engaged in their duties in the ideal Temple. Once more, in Mal. **3.** 3, the sons of Levi are to be purified that they may offer an offering in righteousness instead of the polluted offering of chap. **1.** 7; whilst Gentiles are described in chap. **1.** 11 as offering incense and an unpolluted offering.

Priests and Levites.

Without dogmatising on such passages we are led by the considerations put forth in previous chapters to interpret most of them in the light of the Epistles; and we may fairly point to the offering of the Gentiles (Rom. 15. 16), to the living sacrifices of the Christian (Rom. 12. 1), to the spiritual sacrifices acceptable through Christ (Heb. 13. 15, 16 ; 1 Pet. 2. 5), and to the kings and priests of the new covenant (Rev. 1. 6), as being foreshadowed in the prophetic word.

All the way through the Old Testament ceremony was counted as important, but mere ceremonialism was regarded as hateful to God. In the parting speeches of Moses, in the words of Samuel, in the 51st Psalm, and in the 1st of Isaiah, the spiritual side of worship comes out strongly, and it is evident that no amount of perfunctory offerings would take the place of a spiritual approach to God.

The 53rd of Isaiah.

The 53rd of Isaiah seems to lift the ceremonial veil. It uses certain technical words to indicate that something pointed to in the Old Covenant was to receive its full significance in the time to come, and was to be embodied in the sacrificial death of "the Servant." Eight out of its twelve verses are quoted in the New Testament, and always with reference to Christ. The Christian interpretation of the chapter is undoubted. But the question may be asked, What has a sacrifice to do with kingship? What right have we to combine these very distinct ideas in one person? The answer seems to be that the true sovereignty of Christ is in the first place a supremacy over men's hearts, and that it is effected not by His being of the lineage of David, but by His sacrificial sin-bearing on the Cross. This is the Gospel for the Jew and Gentile; this is what draws all men to Christ; this is the secret of living and loving allegiance to Him; on this truth the loving appeal of God to all the world is based.

(81)

CHAPTER XI.

THE PROPHETIC USE OF NAMES.

THE origin of names as presented in Scripture is a very *Meaning of names.* interesting one. There is probably more than at first appears in the statement that Adam gave names to the animals. The names answered to certain characteristics in the various creatures, and what Adam saw he represented by certain sounds. In the case of human names it is striking that some in very early days marked not only the circumstances or characteristics of the person named, but some expectation connected with him. Of the first kind would be such names as Adam, Eve, Cain, Seth, and Isaac; of the second, such as Noah (Gen. **5.** 29) and Abraham (Gen. **17.** 5). Jacob's name, and his additional name of Israel, are highly significant; so are the names of Jacob's sons. In many of these cases there is a play on the name, two Hebrew roots rather like one another being brought together in the interpretation. When Pharaoh gave Joseph an Egyptian name it was official rather than personal. The translation of it in the Latin Vulgate, *Salvator Mundi*, is not far from the mark. The name of Moses may really be Egyptian, but it admits of a Hebrew explanation (Exod. **2.** 10). Some names are interesting from a linguistic point of view, as they preserve Hebrew roots which would otherwise have been lost. This is the case with Abraham's name.

It is in the prophetic Scriptures that the force of names comes out most clearly; and the expression "His name shall be called" becomes a formula. Several instances of it are

Isai. 7. 3. to be found in the writings of Isaiah. In chap. **7.** 3 the prophet is instructed to take with him his son, probably a mere "child" (or lad), as he is called in *v.* 16; but he has a notable name, Shear Jashub, *i.e.* a remnant shall return (comp. chap. **10.** 21, 22). Before he came to years of discretion something special was to happen, which is described in *v.* 16. But Isaiah has another son, and before this second lad is old enough to speak, certain other events were to take place, and he is named accordingly. These two sons are called signs and wonders, because they embodied certain promises in their very names (**8.** 18). There is a third son spoken of, who is to be called Immanuel, *i.e.* "God is with us" (Isai. **7.** 14 and **8.** 8, 10). Whose son is this? and when is He to be born? He is not a son of Isaiah, but is associated with the House of David; He is to be born of a virgin; He is to represent the presence of God with His people. The prophet recurs to this marvellous Being in chap. **9.** 6 : " Unto us a child is born, unto us a Son is given." He was to be wonderful in counsel, as God was (comp. chap. **28.** 29) ; He was to be the mighty God (comp. chap. **10.** 21) ; He was also to be the Father or Spring of immortality and the Prince of Peace, and He was to sit on the throne of David for ever. It is impossible to separate these chapters from one another ; they are Messianic. No one fulfilled them in their main elements until "the Word was made flesh," born of a woman, emptying Himself of His glory, and being made in the likeness of man. The entrance of Jesus into human life was the fulfilment of the prophecy in all its parts (comp. Matt. **1.** 18–25 with Luke **1.** 26–37). This Being was to be called the Son of God and the Son of the Highest (Luke **1.** 32, 35). He was also called Jesus, *i.e.* Joshua (Jehovah Saviour), because He was to come on a saving mission. He is further described as the Lord our righteousness (Jer. **23.** 6 ; comp. Isai. **45.** 25 and **46.** 13).

THE PROPHETIC USE OF NAMES.

Another person who was named beforehand was John the Baptist (Luke **1.** 60) ; his name signified "the grace of the Lord." The names of his father and mother also seem significant, the one meaning "the Lord remembers," and the other "the oath of God." The roots of both were introduced in Hebrew into the Song of Zechariah (Luke **1.** 72, 73).*

Other names, local as well as personal, have a prophetic sense, as Jezreel, Ammi, lo-Ammi, Ruchamah, and lo-Ruchamah (Hos. **1.** 4, 6, 9); Hephzibah and Beulah (Isai. **62.** 4); Baali and Ishi (Hos. **2.** 16). These are usually explained in the context. There are also prophetic utterances condensed into names, *e.g.* "the way of holiness" (Isai. **35.** 8), "the city of righteousness" (Isai. **1.** 26), "the border of wickedness" (Mal. **1.** 4), "the city of truth" (Zech. **8.** 3), "the repairer of breaches" (Isai. **38.** 12). The name of Solomon (Peaceable) has special interest attached to it because it was ordered beforehand by God (see 1 Chron. **22.** 9). He is evidently regarded as foreshadowing the greater Son of David who should be the Prince of Peace and King of Salem.

In several passages in the Prophets the Messiah is called "the Branch" (*i.e.* the offshoot) of David. One of the Hebrew words thus used is *Netser* (נצר), which is retained in the name of Nazareth or Branch-town. St. Matthew naturally sees significance in this fact; and certainly it is remarkable that the Lord was called a Nazarene all through His ministry, that the name was put on His cross, and that Christians to this day are called Nazarenes by the followers of the False Prophet.

---

* I take it for granted that this and other songs were originally in Hebrew.

CHAPTER XII.

THE NEW TESTAMENT VIEW OF OLD TESTAMENT PROPHECY.

Quotations from the Old to the New Testament.

THERE are about 600 quotations from the Old Testament to the New, besides constant allusive references. These have been examined and discussed from various points of view, but the question now before us is simply this: Is there a definite and consistent view of Old Testament prediction taken by the teachers and writers of the New Testament? In answering this question we have to remember that the subject lies within narrow limits. Numbers of personal and national prophecies are never referred to in the Christian Books. We have chiefly to do with predictions concerning Christ and His Church and His nation. We must also bear in mind that a certain unity of teaching is to be expected, owing to the fact that our risen Lord explained to His followers the nature of the testimony borne to Him in the Law of Moses, the Prophets, and the Psalms (see Luke 24. 27, 45).

On surveying the quotations and references as a whole, we shall be led to the following conclusions:—

i. The historical events narrated in the Old Testament are regarded as facts, not as myths, in the New.

ii. Stress is frequently laid on the actual words in which these narratives are clothed, as accurate, and in some cases peculiarly expressive.

iii. The Old Testament, though a work of sundry writers and many ages, is regarded as one whole, like many members in one body, all animated and ordered by one spirit.

iv. The doctrinal and theological principles of the Old Testament are regarded as true and authoritative, and of universal application. The human heart and the needs of man are the same in all ages. There is the same God, with the same character, the same hatred of wrong-doing, and the same method of approach. Hence the laws, promises, and warnings, given to Israel, are applicable to all time. The way of justification, the duty of holiness, the relative weight of pride and humility, of self-assertion and meekness, of Divine sovereignty and human responsibility, stand unaltered.

v. The history of Israel is regarded as illustrative and prophetic of the need and nature of Divine intervention. Salvation is always finally from the same source, though its nature and the means of its attainment may vary. Israel is thus a representative or typical nation, in its origin, its history, its bondage, and its deliverance. Its story is prophetic, inasmuch as it is the key to the philosophy of all history. It is also provisional, and there is an anticipation running through it which is fulfilled in Christ.

vi. The attributes and functions of Jehovah may legitimately be regarded as realised and embodied in the Only-begotten Son.

vii. The enemies of Israel are the enemies of God, and the words used of them may be used of the enemies of Christ.

viii. The sufferings and the glory to follow, the *penseroso* and *allegro* of the prophets, are to be traced in the humiliation and exaltation of Christ, and in the persecution and final blessedness of His people.

ix. The persecution and martyrdom of God's faithful servants, the prophets of the Old Testament, point to the suffering of Christ for the sin of the world, and illustrate the position of His followers in relation to suffering.

x. The rites in connexion with the Tabernacle prefigure or illustrate the mode of man's approach to God in Christ, sometimes in the way of analogy, and sometimes in the way of contrast.

xi. Zion, Jerusalem, and the Temple illustrate the position of the redeemed community which is being gradually built up of living stones on the One Foundation of Christ.

xii. It should be added that familiar and striking words of the Old Testament are sometimes adopted, on the principle of accommodation, in a sense which has but a faint analogy with their original purpose, and that in such cases they are not pressed as an argument.

To illustrate these twelve canons of interpretation adopted by Christ and His followers would be to write a book. The enumeration of them is based on a careful study of all the known quotations.*

Harmonious interpretations in the New Testament.

We are brought to the conclusion that there was one uniform method commonly adopted by all the New Testament writers in interpreting and applying the Hebrew Scriptures. It is as if they had all been to one school and had studied under one master. But was it the Rabbinical school to which they had been? Was it to Gamaliel, or to Hillel, or to any other Rabbinical leader that they were indebted? All attainable knowledge of the mode of teaching current in that time gives the negative to the suggestion. The Lord Jesus Christ, and no other, was the original source of the method. In this sense, as in many others, He had come a light into the world. It should be observed, however, that the later Old Testament writers frequently made a similar use of the writings of those prophets who had gone before them and applied their words in much the same way.

---

* These are exhibited in a compact and convenient form for the student in Gough's *New Testament Quotations*, a book which might well be reprinted.

NEW TESTAMENT VIEW OF O.T. PROPHECY. 87

Reverting to the predictive element in the quotations, it is important to notice that identity of phrase does not necessarily imply absolute identity of meaning. We have seen this in studying prophetic forms of thought in the Old Testament (see chap. VII.); and this is specially observable in the case of the Apocalypse. Thus, we naturally compare the two witnesses of Rev. **11.** 4 with the two witnesses of Zech. **4.** 14. The two olive trees are here said to be (*i.e.* to represent) "the two anointed ones that stand by the Lord of the whole earth"; whilst in the Revelation they are called "two olive trees and two candlesticks which stand before the God of the whole earth." The latter passage further brings out the analogy of the two witnesses with Moses and Elijah; for they can turn water into blood, and can shut the heaven so that it does not rain. The two passages thus present strong analogies, and point to a kindred solution in both cases, though the interpreter is not pledged to the conclusion that the persons referred to are identical.

Again, the four coloured horses of Zech. **6.** 1–4 are reproduced in Rev. **6.** 1–8, the vision in the latter case being woven upon the threads of the former; but they point to different, though analogous, events.

Taking the Apocalypse as a whole, there is hardly a figure or vision in it which is not contained in germ in Isaiah, Ezekiel, Daniel, or Zechariah. Probably the study of these Books in his old age had prepared the seer for the visions which had to do with the near or the far future.

Passing over the Messianic passages which have been referred to in previous chapters, attention may be called to the utterances which have to do with the Christian community. St. Paul and St. Peter are sometimes criticised for spiritualising certain passages of Isaiah and other prophets, and are accused of stealing away the promises which belong to

Israel and the Church

the nation as such, and of leaving the threats behind. But Israel, whilst it was a nation was also a church, and the position assumed in the second part of Isaiah is that men were to look forward to a time when there should be a Gentile graft on an Israelitish stock. This seems the only key to the prophecy as a whole, and it is this view which is taken by the writers of the New Testament. The lineal Israel was not necessarily the spiritual Israel (see Rom. 2. 28, 29), but there was a spiritual Israel, which doubtless contained representatives of all the Tribes, and which became the basis of the Church of Christ, and it is to this community that all nations flow.

CHAPTER XIII.

CHRONOLOGICAL PROPHECIES. NOTE ON THE JEWISH YEAR.

IT is sometimes said that predictions are only general forecasts, and are not intended to convey definite information as to dates. It may be so in some cases, but a considerable number exhibit either fixed periods within which certain events will come to pass, or else a sequence of events which will be fulfilled in their order. It is proposed in this chapter to give an outline of both of these series of predictions.

I.

(*a.*) In Gen. **6.** 3 we read, "My Spirit shall not always strive with man, for that he also is flesh; yet his days shall be one hundred and twenty years." Putting aside the question of translation, let us confine ourselves to one point: Does the verse refer to the extent of the time during which the longsuffering of God waited before bringing in the Flood on the ungodly (1 Pet. **3.** 20), or does it refer to the abridgment of man's longevity? Josephus took the latter view; Onkelos, in the Targum, the earlier, saying, "A term of one hundred and twenty years will I give them, if they may be converted." St. Peter's words fall in naturally with this view. If this is the true interpretation, then Noah was four hundred and eighty years old when the Divine decision was declared, and Lamech had one hundred and fifteen years yet to live, and both must have known what was shortly to come to pass.

Direct chronological prophecies.

(*b.*) In Gen. **15**. 13 (Acts **7**. 6, 7) we have a term of four hundred years, or four generations, given in a notable revelation of the future. Abraham was now about eighty-five, yet he is told that he should inherit the land (Gen. **13**. 14–17). His child is yet unborn, but his seed is to go into bondage. The place is not specified, but the period is. After four hundred years (in round numbers) the seed should be brought forth. One cause of this delay concerning the inheritance is said to be that the iniquity of the Amorites was not yet filled up (comp. Matt. **23**. 32); but at the close of this long period it would be full. Turning to Exod. **12**. 40 we are told that the sojourn of Israel in Egypt had been four hundred and thirty years. The passage is so worded that it seems written with reference to the old utterance in Genesis, though chronologists are not all of one mind as to the interpretation of the verse, partly owing to the rendering of the LXX. Many believe that the promise to Abraham starts from the date of the original utterance. If so, it takes us first to the death of Joseph, which gives a period of about two hundred and ninety years. Four generations might be taken as either four hundred years or four hundred and eighty years (one hundred and twenty years being then, perhaps, an average of life), and at this reckoning the four hundred and thirty years of Exod. **12**. 40 would come in the midst of the fourth generation. This seems to be the view taken by St. Paul in Gal. **3**. 17, where he says that the Sinaitic covenant was four hundred and thirty-years after the Abrahamic; and according to it the actual period of affliction from the time of Joseph's death to the Exodus would be about two centuries, inclusive of eighty years from Moses' birth to his call. Although interpreters are not sure as to the dates referred to, yet the prophecy is manifestly chronological in its intent.

CHRONOLOGICAL PROPHECIES. 91

(*c.*) Num. **14.** 33, "Your children shall wander in the desert forty years." This period was fixed in connexion with the forty days spent in searching the Land of Canaan. The postponement to Israel was a prolongation of opportunity to the Canaanites, and probably fitted in with the invasion of Palestine by the hornet, *i.e.* perhaps by Egypt.* The prediction in this case was clearly fulfilled.

Passing over the prediction of the fall of Jericho on the seventh day (Josh. **6.** 5), and the addition of fifteen years to Hezekiah's age (2 Kings **20.** 6), we turn to the Prophetic Books.

(*d.*) Jonah **3.** 4, "Within forty days Nineveh shall be destroyed."—The number forty is of frequent occurrence as a round number. But in this case the very book which tells us of the prediction tells us also that it was not fulfilled (see *supra*, chap. IV.). God was not slack concerning His threat, but He gave heed to the national (even though sadly superficial) repentance; and the judgment was postponed.

(*e.*) Isai. **7.** 8, "Within sixty-five years Ephraim shall be broken."—This was uttered in the reign of Ahaz; and sixty-five years after the first year of Ahaz the Captivity of the Northern Kingdom was completed.

(*f.*) Isai. **16.** 14.—Three years were allotted to Moab. Compare Isai. **20.** 3, where three years were given as a sign to Egypt and Cush; and Isai. **21.** 16, where one year was given to Kedar.

(*g.*) Isai. **23.** 15-17, "For seventy years Tyre shall be forgotten."—Subsequently it was to be restored. No date is given. Seventy may be a round number; in fact, a generation, for generations had dwindled down to threescore and ten years.

---

* The bee was the hieroglyphic sign of Lower Egypt; and the hornet may have been substituted for it in the enigmatical language of prophecy.

(*h*.) Ezek. **29**. 11–13.—Egypt was to be desolate forty years, and then restored. The date of the utterance is fixed (circ. B.C. 487). The language is clear and definite. Perhaps some historical illustration of it may yet be forthcoming.

(*i*.) Jer. **25**. 11, 12.—Seventy years are allotted to the Babylonian domination over Judah and its neighbours, who were to be destroyed (*i.e.* brought low).

(*j*.) Jer. **29**. 10.—Seventy years were to be the term of Judah's Captivity. The letter enclosing this prediction was sent to Babylon after the second captivity, *i.e.* that in which Ezekiel was carried away (circ. B.C. 600—598), but the reckoning in years is generally taken from the first captivity (B.C. 606). The period of what may be called seventy years penal servitude was fixed by the number of neglected sabbatical years during the whole time of the kings (Lev. **26**. 34, 35; 2 Chron. **36**. 21); and when the seventy years had run out, Daniel, who had been in Chaldea and Persia all the time, prayed for the fulfilment of God's promise (Dan. **9**. 3).

(*k*.) The prophecies in Daniel are highly chronological. In Dan. **4**. 16, 23, 25, 32 we have reference to a period of "seven times." This expression is sometimes taken by students as parallel with Lev. **26**. 18, etc., but this view can hardly be accurate; for in Leviticus the word שֶׁבַע means simply "seven," *i.e.* seven-fold; but in Daniel the Chaldee expression signifies "seven periods," whether days, months, or years. The fulfilment of the prediction came a year later, *i.e.* "at the end of twelve months" (*v.* 29); and "at the end of the days" the king's reason returned to him. Why do commentators always suppose that the "times" in this passage were years?

(*l*.) In Dan. **7**. 25 and **12**. 7 we have reference to "a time, times, and a half time," the former of these passages is in Chaldee, and the latter in Hebrew, but the word for "time" in both passages stands for "an appointed period." In the one case the period marks the duration of the affliction of God's people at the hand of the eleventh Power (the little horn), and in the other the same period is described as "the scattering of the holy people." It is followed by the Judgment.

This period is reproduced in the Book of the Revelation in three forms. First, we have the expression "a time, times, and half a time" (Rev. **12.** 14), where it refers to a period of wilderness life or desolation for the "woman." Secondly, it is put into days (1,260) in verse 6, in the same context; and we find the same period appointed for the prophesying of the two witnesses (chap. **11.** 3). Lastly, it appears as forty-two months in chap. **11.** 2, and is applied to the treading down of the Holy City. It seems clear that 1,260 days are the same as forty-two months of thirty days each, and that they make up three and a half years. And the sense of these passages so fits in with the two in Daniel mentioned above that we naturally take the whole series together as representing one period, without determining whether the days are literal days or whether each day stands for a year, as in Ezekiel's vision (Ezek. **4.** 4–9).

(*m.*) Dan. **8.** 14.—Here the period of treading down and desolation or wilderness life is called 2,300 days, but the Hebrew word used for day is a compound one, signifying "evening-morning." The vision in this chapter is distinct from the rest, and may refer to a different historical event. Some students think that the compound word points to literal rather than ideal days; but this view is not usually taken.

(*n.*) In Dan. **12.** 11, 12 we have a period of 1,290 days which begin with the setting up of the Abomination of Desolation; also there is an additional thirty-five days, which gives what has been called the *ne plus ultra* of prophecy, nothing more being revealed as to time. If these days are years, and if the setting up of the Abomination of Desolation is to be associated with the siege of Jerusalem by the Romans (comp. Matt. **24.** 15 with Luke **21.** 20), then the prediction will not be fulfilled for four more centuries.

(*o.*) The chronological prophecy of Dan. **9** stands over for consideration. It deals with a period of seventy weeks. But the word translated "week" does not necessarily mean a week of days, and the word "day" does not occur in the prophecy. The passage is very condensed, and some points in the translation and application are open to question. It naturally attracted the attention of Sir Isaac Newton, and his interpretation deserves respectful study. A period of seventy times seven was "determined" (*lit.* "notched") in the mind of the Eternal. From the restoration of the City (not the Temple) to Messiah the Prince was to be seven times seven and sixty-two times seven. It is natural to take these as "sevens" or "weeks" of years, *i.e.* 483 years, because if they had been weeks of days they would probably have been called so (see chap. **10.** 2). Here, then, we have a determined period which began long after Daniel's death, and must be fixed by Neh. **2** as circ. B.C. 444. The Julian method of computing years was not in use then; but according to the Jewish mode of reckoning, the period here indicated would run out in about A.D. 25, when, according to Mark **1.** 15, the Lord Jesus proclaimed, "The time is fulfilled, and the kingdom of God has drawn nigh."* Compare Gal. **4.** 4, where the fulness or fulfilment of the time is again referred to.

There is a period of seven years still standing over to complete the seventy times seven years. This seems to include

---

* See note at the end of the chapter on the Jewish year.

the time from the Messiah till the fall of Jerusalem. But we see, as a matter of history, that it was protracted; for while the Lord died and rose again at the half week, *i.e.* circ. A.D. 29-30, the other half, which would naturally have closed about A.D. 33, was extended till A.D. 70. This prolongation was not slackness, but mercy. It was a gracious extension; but alas! the mass of the people remained unchanged; and the city fell. There was a terrible three and a half years later, however, in connexion with the great rising under Bar-Cochab (A.D. 130). Hippolytus (circ. A.D. 200) considers that this three and a half years will come at the end of the present age, when antichrist will be manifested and destroyed. (See his work on *Christ and Antichrist*, § 43).

(*p.*) In the New Testament there are a few chronological prophecies, notably those that predict the resurrection of Christ in three days. The period is said to be analogous with that of the entombment of Jonah (Matt. **12.** 40). This remarkable event accounts for the expression in Hos. **6.** 2 : "After two days He will revive us; in the third day He will raise us up"; for Hosea lived shortly after the time of Jonah (comp. 2 Kings **14.** 25 with Hos. **1.** 1). As the three days and three nights in our Lord's case were shortened, so it may be that Jonah's entombment was shorter than we naturally suppose. The anticipation of Hosea concerning Israel was fulfilled in Christ, as was the case with an earlier stage of Israel's history (comp. Hos. **11.** 1 with Matt. **2.** 15).

(*q.*) In the Apocalypse we have not only the passages concerning the three and a half years already referred to, but also the vision of the thousand years (Rev. **20.** 2-7). The fact that this long period is mentioned six times gives it a certain fixity and definiteness, and thus distinguishes it from the ideal and comparative expression of Ps. **90.** 4 and 2 Pet. **3.** 8. It apparently points to the truth that the period so often looked forward to as "the Day of the Lord" is measured out as an actual thousand years. This was the conviction of the early Church, but that community could not possibly tell how long a period was to come first—a period obscurely intimated by St. Paul in 2 Thess. **2**, and by the Seer of the Apocalypse under the expression "a time and times and half a time"; nor could they decide how long a period would come after the thousand years.

II.

Indirect chronological prophecies.

The above are the most notable of the direct measuring of the distance of future events; and we have now to consider the indirect chronological prophecies, *i.e.* those that have to do with the sequence of events rather than with the fixed number of years which those events involve.

(*a.*) Gen. **49.** 10, "The sceptre shall not depart from Judah nor one who issues decrees from between his feet (*i.e.* from his family) until Shiloh comes; and unto him shall the obedience of the peoples be."—The explanation of the Targums is: "Kings shall not cease from the House of Judah . . . until the time that the King Messiah shall come, Whose is the kingdom, and to Whom all the kingdoms of the earth shall be obedient." The first point to notice is the implied prediction that the sceptre was to get into the hands of Judah. This did not take place till the time of David. From his time onward, in spite even of the Captivity, Judah remained the ruling tribe and Jerusalem the metropolis; moreover, the Davidic dynasty was kept up through the kingly period, and is traceable onward through Zorobabel, and reappears in Joseph, the adopted and reputed father of the Lord Jesus. But the prophecy gives also a *terminus ad quem*. What should happen *after* Shiloh came? We know what did happen. Jerusalem was destroyed, Judah was desolated, and the Jews were scattered. The only sense in which Judah has held the sceptre is in the establishment of the Kingdom of Christ, "the Lion of the Tribe of Judah" (Rev. **5.** 5), Who is still winning the obedience of the peoples. These broad facts stand out clear, and relieve us of the necessity of discussing too narrowly the original meaning of the word Shiloh. Spelt as it stands in Hebrew it may signify the Rest-giver (comp. Matt. **11.** 28, 29); but by changing the last letter from h (ה) to v (ו) we are reminded of Ezekiel's words (chap. **21.** 27), which may be a reference to the prophecy (with a slight play upon the words), "Until He come whose right it is."

(*b.*) Isai. **8. 4,** "For before the child shall have knowledge to cry father and mother, the riches of Damascus and the spoil of Samaria shall be taken away before the king of Assyria."

Compare Isai. **7.** 16, "For before the child shall have knowledge to refuse the evil and to choose the good, the land by whose two kings thou art agitated shall be forsaken."

The first of these passages refers to Isaiah's second child, Maher-shalal-hash-baz, and the second to his first child, Shear Jashub. The two must be interpreted on the same lines; and we can see the fulfilment by comparing 1 Kings **16** with 2 Chron. **28.** But they are associated with the promise of a virgin-born Son to the House of David, whose name should be Immanuel, and whose functions are further described in Isai. **9** and **11.** The group of chapters from the 7th to the 12th are to be taken together, and form an excellent illustration of the intermingling of foreground and background. It is strange to see the restlessness of some students under the words uttered concerning the virgin-born Being Who was to combine the natural and supernatural in His birth as He did certainly in His life. The LXX. found no difficulty in the word "virgin," and there is nothing in the six other passages where the word occurs to justify the difficulty. The highly wrought imagination of those who think that the forthcoming son might be Hezekiah is shattered by the plain fact that Hezekiah was at least ten years old at the time! Nor is there anything in the nature of things which should render the fact disclosed in the prophecy unfitting. The law of fertility imposed on our first parents did not apply to their own origin; and if there was a special provision or a special generative act in the case of the First Adam, who after all was only a man, why should it be thought incredible that there should be something special in the case of the Second Adam, who, according to all New Testament teaching, came from above, though born of a woman?

(*c.*) Joel 2.—The order in this chapter is important because of the use made of it in the New Testament. After describing the locust-hordes, the prophet urges the people to call upon the Lord; then He drives away the enemy; the land rejoices; faith revives; afterwards (*v.* 28) the Spirit is poured out; signs and portents accompany or follow; the great and terrible day of the Lord, to which Malachi subsequently refers (4. 5), comes; there is deliverance in Zion and among the remnant whom the Lord shall call.

(*d.*) Amos 9. 8.—The sinful kingdom is to be destroyed, but not utterly. In that day (*i.e.* after the dispersion) the house of David is to be re-established (Acts 15. 16, 17) and the people restored for ever.

(*e.*) Micah 3. 12 and 4. 1, 2.—Jerusalem and Zion are to be ruinous heaps; but the latter days will usher in a time when Jerusalem and Zion become a centre of light and peace among the nations. The remnant becomes a strong nation and the Lord reigns over them for ever. And who is to be the actual ruler? One born at Bethlehem (5. 2); and in Him the old promises made to Abraham will be fulfilled (7. 20).

(*f.*) Dan. **2.**—There is an orderly sequence of world-empires : Babylonian, Persian, Greek, Roman. Each of these grew up out of its predecessor and occupied common ground to a large extent, though with a westward tendency. The stone falls on the feet, *i.e.* on the subdivisions of the Roman Empire. This, as Dr. Pusey points out in his work on Daniel, is yet to be accomplished.

(*g.*) In Matt. **24**, Mark **13**, and Luke **21**, we have three accounts of our Lord's programme with regard to the future of Jerusalem and His own coming (in one sense ; see *supra*, chap. VIII.) ; and we are told (Luke **21.** 24) that Jerusalem was to be trodden down by the Gentiles until the times of the Gentiles be fulfilled ; and it may fairly be implied that when those times are fulfilled there would be an uprising of Jerusalem and a national restoration, which should be as life from the dead. This utterance fits in with several passages in the Old Testament. As there are three or four definite references to Daniel in the Lord's programme, we naturally turn to Daniel to see if we can find light on this matter. In chap. **8.** 13, 14 the question is asked "How long shall be the vision concerning the daily sacrifice and the transgression of desolation to give both the sanctuary and the host (*i.e.* the people) to be trodden under foot ? " And the answer is given, " Unto two thousand three hundred evening-mornings ; then shall the sanctuary be cleansed." It is at least possible that we have here the duration of the times of the Gentiles. If we take these evening-mornings as days, the period would amount to a little less than seven years. This view does not adjust itself to anything. If we take them as years, we see that the prediction covers a long period which has not yet run out.

(*h.*) Luke **21.** 32, "This generation shall not pass till all be fulfilled."—This prediction is not of universal bearing, but must be limited to its subject-matter, which is the coming of the Lord to visit Jerusalem for its sins, and to inaugurate the times of the Gentiles. There were some young people standing round the Lord who would see both the treading down of Jerusalem and the spread of the Kingdom of Christ far and wide.

(*i.*) Rom. **11**. 25, " Partial blindness has befallen Israel until the fulness of the Gentiles be come in ; and so all Israel (*i.e.* Israel as a whole) shall be saved, or restored."—This is both a national and a spiritual Restitution. Compare Acts **3**. 19–21, where St. Peter calls on Israel to repent and return that their sins might be blotted out, and so the Lord might send forth Jesus the Messiah, Whom the heavens must retain until the times of the Restitution of all the things of which the prophets had spoken from of old.

(*j.*) 1 Cor. **15**. 23.—Here we have a distinct order with regard to the Resurrection, " Christ the First-fruits." That is past. Then " those that belong to Christ at His coming." " Then the end " ; that is the final dispensation which has been looked forward to for so long a time. The last and crowning triumph of Christ is the overcoming of death. After this Christ will be seen not as a King, but as a Son Who has been acting throughout in obedience to His Father.

(*k.*) 1 Thess. **4**. 14–17.—Another order connected with the Lord's appearing. The Lord comes down ; the dead in Christ rise ; then the saints who have not died are caught up with them to meet the Lord in the air, and to be ever with the Lord.

(*l.*) 2 Thess. **1**. 6–9.—Tribulation is to come to the troubler, and rest to the troubled ; and these events synchronise with the revelation of the Lord Jesus, whose work " in that day " is two-fold. He will both take vengeance on the disobedient and be glorified in His saints.

(*m.*) 2 Thess. **2**. 2, etc.— Some thought that " the day " had set in already (see R.V.). This was a mistake. There must

Note on the Jewish Year.

A solar year is about 365¼ days. A lunar year is about 354 days. This was pointed out by the celebrated Julius Africanus (circ. A.D. 220) when discussing the seventy weeks. The ideal year used in Dan. 7. 25 and 12. 7, also in Rev. 11 and 12, is 360 days. The last is generally supposed to be the Chaldean and Assyrian year. It was perhaps originally the Israelite year also; and from this we have derived the division of the circle into 360 degrees. Our ordinary chronology for ancient times follows the arrangement ordered by Julius Cæsar (B.C. 45), who made the sun's course the standard. His twelve months were alternately thirty and thirty-one days, except February, which was twenty-nine. This, however, gets us a day wrong every 130 years. Pope Gregory XIII. rectified the existing error by deducting ten days from October 1582, and thus bringing the vernal equinox back to March 21. In order to avoid further errors he ordered that the last year of each century, though naturally divisible by four, should not be a leap-year in the case of three out of every four centuries. Hence it came to pass that the year 1900 was not a leap-year. England adopted this new style in 1752. The Mohammedans have a better system than ours, and by it an error of a day can only be made in the course of 5,000 years.

The Jewish year is partly lunar, for it consists naturally of twelve months, of which half have thirty days each, and the other half have twenty-nine. The year starts from the first appearance of the moon in Nisan. Being, however, so far behind the solar year, to which it had to adapt itself for the purpose of the season-feasts, an additional month is thrown in once in every three years, and is called *Ve-adar*, *i.e.* an additional (month of) *Adar*. Julius Africanus said that in his time the Jews inserted three intercalary months every eight years. A good deal of our ancient Eastern chronology must be affected by the question of the length of the year in vogue; and perhaps some of the dates will need considerable correction. For example, 1,260 of the years which reckon 360 days to a year if compared with the same number of Julian years show a difference of about eighteen years; and 475 Julian years make 490 lunar years. A comparative calendar of ancient times is a sore *desideratum* for historical and prophetic students.

It has been pointed out that the years from Nehemiah to Christ, if reckoned on the Jewish calculation of 354 days to a year, bring us to about A.D. 25. But this calculation ignores the intercalary month which the Jews have to throw in once in three years. If we added in those months the date of the manifestation of the Messiah would be a few years later. But it is doubtful if the Jewish calculators would take in these additional months. At any rate, the period given in Daniel runs out in the age of the mission of Christ, and there must have been some studious Jews who were looking for Him just at the time in which He was manifested.

Dr. Anderson, in his *Coming Prince* (2nd ed., 1882, p. 127), works out the problem thus:—"What was the length of the period intervening between the issuing of the decree to rebuild Jerusalem and the public advent of Messiah the Prince, *i.e.* between the 14th March B.C. 445 and the 6th April A.D. 32? The interval contained exactly, to the very day, 173,880 days, or seven times sixty-nine prophetic years of 360 days, the first

THE JEWISH YEAR.

sixty-nine weeks of Gabriel's prophecy." By the public advent of the Prince Dr. Anderson understands the triumphal entry into Jerusalem. His view of the date deserves consideration, though it varies by two or three years from the views of others. The materials for fixing exact dates seem hardly yet in our hands.

The "year-day" theory, as applicable to parts of Daniel and the Revelation, and perhaps to other prophecies, is tacitly accepted by most prophetic students. Elliott discusses it at length in the 3rd volume of his *Horæ Apocalypticæ*.

Whether an "hour" is to be taken as a twenty-fourth part of a year-day is not quite so clear (see, *e.g.* Rev. 9. 15). The Rev. W. Girdlestone, in his *Observations on Daniel* (1820), says, "I have deviated from a calculation of Bishop Newton, who considers an hour as the measure of fifteen days or the twenty-fourth part of a year, supposing that the Jews divided their day as we do into twenty-four hours; but the fact is that their nights were measured by watches, and their days, or the space between sunrise and sunset, by hours, which were twelve; a prophetic hour then is the 12th part of a prophetic day, and is consequently a month."

For convenience in studying the history of the past in connexion with prophecy a list of the most noteworthy historic dates is given on page 181.

CHAPTER XIV.

METHODS OF STUDYING PROPHECY. NOTE ON THE STRUCTURE OF THE APOCALYPSE.

Study of the text.

THERE is no royal road to the scientific study of prophecy. We have to begin with words and sentences before we launch into ideas. We are dealing with a Semitic tongue, with Oriental illustrations, usually with poetry which abounds in brevities, obscurities, and rarities of expression, and above all we have before us not the story of the past, but the revelation of the future. As we face the text and pore over its words we ask ourselves how they would have been understood at the time, and on what ground we modify or enlarge their meaning. For example, Who were the "saints" in the days of Daniel, and who are the "saints" in the Revelation and kindred books? Is there anything in the Christian system answering to the " daily sacrifice " which Daniel describes as to be taken away? How far is the language of hyperbole, so frequent in Isaiah, to be toned down by the accommodating spirit of St. Paul, and how far will it yet receive a literal fulfilment in accordance with the pictorial language of the Apocalypse. The New Testament adopts the older prophecies to its needs, but does not profess to absorb them. The time of Restitution which all the prophets had in their minds has not yet come (see Acts **3.** 21). Christians by virtue of their union with Christ become fellow-heirs with Israel; but they must not filch away the old promises which belong to the children of Abraham and leave them nothing but the threats. The chapter-headings in the Authorised Version have a good deal to answer for, and some of our expositors have followed in their wake;

METHODS OF STUDYING PROPHECY. 105

and this undoubtedly has caused much soreness in the mind of the Jew.

In a word, watchful care and accuracy in dealing with words, fidelity to the text, thorough study of the historical books which set forth God in Providence, an honest determination to be led by the Spirit of Truth and not by a foregone theory—these are the requirements of the man who would deal thoroughly and loyally with the prophetic Scriptures.

In entering upon his task the scientific student of Biblical prophecy has two methods before him. He may take each Book separately and examine and analyse its contents sentence by sentence; or he may trace certain subjects through the Bible as a whole. It seems wisest to study Books first and subjects afterwards.

I.

In dealing with the Books the question of their date has to be considered, for they have to be studied, so far as possible, in chronological order and in connexion with the history of the times in which they were written. Indications of the writer's date were usually given at the beginning of his Book; and in the longer Books several of the special utterances are dated. Occasionally where no date is given we may find some clue to the writer's age in his language, his allusions to current events, or the use he makes of his predecessors' works. Speaking generally, the dated Prophetic Books of the Old Testament (putting aside the Psalms) fall into three groups. First, there are the men of Hezekiah's age, including Jonah, Amos, Hosea, Micah, and Isaiah. Secondly, there are the men of Josiah's age, including Zephaniah, Jeremiah, and Ezekiel. The first of these periods covers the captivity of Israel, and the second the captivity of Judah. The third group covers the age of the Restoration, including Daniel, Haggai, and Zechariah. The

Study of Books.

Groups of prophets.

prophecies of Obadiah, Joel, Nahum, and Habakkuk are undated, but probably come between the first and second periods. Daniel, being partly historical and partly prophetical, and being (as a Book) anonymous, is associated in the Jewish arrangement of the Bible with the later histories. It covers the ground from the Captivity to the Restoration. Malachi is generally supposed, on traditional and internal grounds, to be contemporary with Nehemiah.

Those who reject the definite predictive element in Scripture have their own methods of elimination and explanation, which are not under discussion here. Undoubtedly at first sight there would seem reasons for bringing down the last twenty-seven chapters of Isaiah into the second of the groups named above, and for pushing back some of the later chapters of Zechariah into the first group; but in both cases if we had a little more knowledge of the times we might see cause to adhere to the traditional view, in favour of which the last word has not yet been said. The references in Zechariah to Assyria do not necessarily imply that the Assyrian rule was then dominant over the East any more than the references in the Revelation to Babylon imply the same of the Babylonian Empire. The future is expressed in terms of the past (see chap. IX., *supra*). Reverting for a moment to the case of Isaiah, we have to remember the old Hebrew tradition that the prophet was slain in his old age by order of Manasseh, and that Manasseh himself was carried captive to Babylon under Esarhaddon. Even in Hezekiah's time Babylon was a power to be considered, but it was still more conspicuous in Manasseh's time. The magnificent and stirring chapters of which we speak, and which are theological rather than political in their atmosphere, may have been written, perhaps from prison, in the light of coming national troubles and in the prospect of the time promised as far back as Lev. **26**,

Isaiah.

METHODS OF STUDYING PROPHECY.

when the people should bear the punishment of their iniquity and should be restored. This would be the "foreground," while the "middle-distance" has to do with the rise of Christianity, and the "back-ground" or "horizon" is occupied with the prospect of the new heavens and the new earth.

Subdivisions of Books. Having thus got a general idea of the date of the writer, we naturally consider the subject-matter and characteristics of each Book, and its main subdivisions; disregarding the divisions into chapters in some cases (see, *e.g.* Dan. **10** and **11**); we study the Book in portions according to the nature of their contents. In some cases, *e.g.* Haggai, each prophecy has its own date, and we can read it in the light of contemporary history; but in others, *e.g.* Joel, we hardly know whether we have a single utterance or a group of two or three messages. The groups in Isaiah are fairly discernible, and are in fairly consecutive order, but this is not the case in Jeremiah.

Quotations. Having mastered, so far as possible, the history of the age in which each prophet lived, and the leading subjects of his Book, our next course is to read it by the light of the quotations which it makes from its predecessors, and of the use made of it in the later Books of the Hebrew Scriptures and in the New Testament. To study the prophets without reference to Christ seems as unscientific as to study the body without reference to the head. The Spirit of Christ was in the Prophets all the way through (1 Pet. **1.** 11), and each Book is to be read as part of a great whole.

Utterances. Pursuing our investigations we give ourselves more carefully to the detailed utterances of the Book in our hands, asking various questions as we read, *e.g.* :—

    i. What part is historic, and what predictive?
    ii. What part is visionary, and what real?
    iii. What is figurative, and what literal?
    iv. What utterances are conditional, and what absolute?

v. What parts have been fulfilled since the prophecy was written, either sooner or later, and what still remain unfulfilled?

vi. What belongs to the Northern Kingdom, and what to the Southern?

vii. What is for outside nations, and what for the world at large?

viii. What is earthly, and what is heavenly?

ix. What is, in a more or less definite sense, Messianic?

Every student will see the advantage of studying the fulfilled before the unfulfilled, the easy before the obscure, the foreground before the background. He thus builds on a sure foundation, advancing from step to step, distinguishing the shadows from the substance, and detecting the main outlines of what is still future by the aid of his accurate study of the past.

II.

Special chapters.

Passing from Books to Subjects, it may be noted that there are certain chapters which may be regarded as keys to prophecy, either because they present a prophetic scheme in outline, or because they call special attention to subjects of surpassing interest. The following may be enumerated, though each which is named suggests kindred chapters calling for attentive study:—

Gen. **12**, The original promises made to Abraham and his seed.

Gen. **49**, Containing the Blessing of the Tribes by Jacob.

Lev. **26**, and Deut. **28**, Containing the promises and threats set before the people when they were about to enter Canaan.

Deut. **32**, The prophetic song, which gives the scheme of Israel's fall and rising again through all time.

Isai. **13, 14**, The fall of Babylon and the restoration of Israel.

Isai. **24—27**, The Restitution of all things.

Isai. **53**, The Sin-bearer.

Ezek. **38, 39**, The troubles of the latter days.

Dan. **2, 7**, The rise and fall of Empires.

Dan. **9**, The seventy weeks.

Zech. **12—14**, The downfall of the adversaries of Jerusalem.

Matt. **24, 25**, The Lord's utterance concerning His coming.

Rom. **9—11**, The prospects of Israel.

Rev. **20—22**, Closing scenes in the world's history.

It will be observed that these prophecies of Scripture, of which those just enumerated are special samples, have to do with persons, with dynasties, with nations, and with the world. Among them we find predictions which concern Abraham, Joseph, the Baptist, and the Messiah. So there are predictions which concern the dynasty of David and the line of Jehu. There are prophecies concerning Syria, Edom, Arabia, Moab, Ammon, Tyre, Zidon, Philistia, Egypt, Ethiopia, Assyria, Babylon, Persia, Greece, Rome, as well as Israel. Lastly, there are the utterances concerning the second coming of Christ to save and to judge the world, and those which announce the resurrection of the dead and the establishment of a new order of things.

In the remaining chapters of this book, only a few of the most notable of these topics will be touched upon, with a view of determining, so far as possible, the best method of dealing with them. No attempt is made to give a complete and detailed interpretation of prophecy, and perhaps more questions will be raised than can be answered; but the statement of problems is sometimes instructive and leads the way to further detailed but cautious enquiry.

Note on the Structure of the Apocalypse.

Characteristics of the Apocalypse.

This Book is made up of a series of visions usually introduced by the formula "And I saw." They are closely related to one another, the earlier frequently referring by anticipation to the later. With regard to their arrangement the question constantly rises whether some of the visions are descriptions of contemporary events, being narrated one after the other through the necessity of language, as in the narratives concerning contemporary kings of Israel and Judah, or whether they are consecutive; and, if the latter is the case, whether allowance is to be made for the possibility of long gaps between some of the visions, as in the case of the visions of Daniel.

Schools of students.

The English historical school has been ably represented in modern times by such men as Elliott, Garratt, and Guinness, who see in the visions associated with the Seals, the Trumpets, and the Vials, an outline of God's dealings with the Church and with Israel till the "time of the end," which we are rapidly approaching, though they differ from each other in some particulars.[*] The Preterist school consider that the larger portion of the Book received its fulfilment in the earliest ages of the Church; whilst the Futurists hold that the Book as a whole refers to the time of the end.

Relation to Old Testament.

Considering how much of the groundwork of the Book is due to the writings of Isaiah, Ezekiel, Daniel, and Zechariah, we see the impossibility of regarding it as an absolutely independent production. The visions granted to St. John were evidently presented in figures taken from

---

[*] See Birks' excellent summary on the Structure of the Apocalypse written after fifty years' study of the subject in his *Thoughts on Sacred Prophecy* (Hodder, 1880).

the writings of these four great men which the Seer had no doubt studied enthusiastically either before or during his time of seclusion in Patmos.

One notable feature of the Book is the reiteration of the mystical number *Seven* in it. The word occurs over fifty times. It is applied to lamps, *i.e.* churches; to torches, *i.e.* spirits; to stars, *i.e.* angels; to seals; to heads, *i.e.* mountains; to eyes, *i.e.* spirits; also to trumpets, thunders, thousands, crowns, plagues, vials, kings. This phenomenon is the more remarkable owing to the fact that the number Seven is never so much as named in St. John's Gospel or in any of the Epistles at all, except in Heb. **11.** 30, which is a purely incidental reference. Some of these sevens can be traced in the Old Testament; for we have seven-fold vengeance (Gen. **4.** 15; Lev. **26.** 18), seven trumpets blown before the fall of Jericho (Josh. **6.** 4, etc.), seven shepherds (Mic. **5.** 5), seven eyes (Zech. **3.** 9), and seven lamps (Exod. **37.** 23; Zech. **4.** 2).*

It is remarkable how little "local colouring" there is in the Book. If we had not been told that it was written by an exile in Patmos, we should not have found it out, though the references to the sea-shore might have struck us as noteworthy. There is nothing clearly indicative of a date, and it is still open to conjecture whether the Book was written in the age of Nero or of Domitian, though the testimony of early writers is so strong for the later date (circ. A.D. 95) that it may be regarded as still in possession. Had the great blow fallen upon Jerusalem, or had it not? Had "the woman" fled into the wilderness? Were the Apostles still living, or had other personages stepped into their place? It seems as if the letters to the seven Churches

Local colouring.

---

* The expression "Seven Stars" of Amos 5. 8, A.V., is not a case in point. The Hebrew word כימה simply means a heap or cluster, and the Pleiades are referred to. See R.V.

afford the only materials for enquiry into these questions; and the references in them to false teaching and evil practices appear to point to a later rather than an earlier date.

Authorship. Even the authorship of the Book is wrapped in mystery. The fragments of Papias would lead us to suppose that there were two notable Johns at that time, John the Apostle and John the Presbyter. The writer of the Gospel and of the first Epistle (which is a practical application of the Gospel) never names himself, but we know who he was. The writer of the Second and Third Epistles of St. John calls himself the Elder. The writer of the Apocalypse calls himself John the servant of the Lord; but there is an apostolic atmosphere about him, and in spite of the verbal peculiarities of the book (which may best be accounted for by consideration of the subject and of the Old Testament materials which were used) there seems to be no sufficient reason for doubting that the author is the disciple* whom Jesus loved, which was the view of the early Church.

The whole Book claims to be a faithful report of what John had actually seen in vision. The events recorded were to come to pass quickly (1. 1-3, and **22.** 6, 7). The Book was written to a little cluster of Christian Communities in the west of Asia Minor, though doubtless intended to be spread far and wide. The needs of these seven Communities are primarily considered, and the threats and promises announced are in terms most of which are explained in *The opening.* later parts of the book. After this preliminary and solemn call on the Churches to listen, the Revelation proper begins with a glimpse of the spirit-world and the unrolling of

---

* It is strange that the word "disciple" only occurs in the Gospels and Acts. The history of the word "apostle" is still more remarkable. It is only found once in the first, second, and fourth gospels; frequently in St. Luke and Acts, habitually by St. Paul. The references in Rev. 2. 2; 18. 20; 21. **14** are interesting.

THE APOCALYPSE.

the seven-sealed book by the Lamb. As the seals are opened one by one, a time of warfare, with its usual accompaniments, together with persecution and its due recompense, is portrayed, whilst the "sealed" of Israel and of the Gentile world enter into their rest and joy. As soon as the last seal is broken the whole Book of Revelation may be regarded as unfolded before the Seer's eye, and he proceeds to tell what he saw. It appears from what he saw that a series of judgments would follow the trumpet sounds of the seven angels, the last of which would indicate the end (**11. 15**). The events portrayed seemed at first sight to be consecutive, both in order and in time, but they are broken into, first by an intervening series which John was forbidden to write down (**10. 4**), and secondly by the times of the Gentiles (**11. 2**, etc.), so that the *Parousia** which had been speedily anticipated is delayed.

At this stage, *i.e.* at the end of the 11th chapter, the first great scene or series of scenes presented on the complete opening of the Book appears to be brought to a close. Looking, however, in another direction, the Seer perceives the desolation of Israel during the times of the Gentiles, together with the persecution of the Christian community, all carried on under the instigation of Satan through the agency of the imperial Beast and his clever and deceptive ally or representative (chaps. **12** and **13**). Words of encouragement are uttered to those who suffer for Christ in those evil times (**14. 1-13**), and attention is afterwards called to the vision of judgment on the persecuting and ungodly power (**14. 14—19. 21**). Then follow the Millennium and the subsequent outbreak (**20. 1-10**), together with the post-millennial judgment.

The second portion.

---

* This word does not occur in the Revelation, but it is implied in chap. 11. 15, &c.

The third portion.

Here the second great phase of the Future draws to a close. But there is yet a third series of visions or scenes included in the opened book; it is the vision of the Bride— a vast spiritual community gathered from Jewish and Gentile sources forming a great living edifice (comp. Eph. **2**. 19–22 ; 1 Pet. **2**. 4–10). Amongst other remarkable things uttered concerning the community, we read that the nations of the saved shall walk in the light of it (**21.** 24), while the unclean and abominable and the liar are excluded from its benefit (**21.** 27 ; comp. **22.** 15). It is not so easy to decide whether this picture refers to the condition of the saints during the Millennium, or to the final condition of things after the establishment of the new heavens and new earth subsequent to the General Judgment. The latter is the natural view, but there are difficulties in it. These are discussed and in part removed in Birks' *Outlines of Unfulfilled Prophecy*. Perhaps what would be true in the one case will also be true in the other in some measure. The language is highly figurative, but the impression produced on the mind is the ultimate and final banishment of evil from God's universe.

Such is a *prima facie* view of this marvellous Book. Taking the analogy of the Book of Daniel it is natural to believe that it refers in part to events following closely on John's time, *i.e.* on the beginning of the 2nd century, and that it furnishes at least some light on the centuries which should intervene before the Consummation. Certainly, it has kept hope alive in the hearts of many during the ages of persecution, whether imperial or ecclesiastical, and will do so till the end.

CHAPTER XV.

PROMISES TO ABRAHAM AND DAVID FULFILLED IN CHRIST.

THE Bible almost begins with a promise (Gen. **3**. 15), and it certainly ends with one (Rev. **22**. 20), and the ultimate fulfilment of the first will adjust itself to the accomplishment of the last. The great historical series of promises lies midway between them, and is ushered in at the call of Abraham. There were three promises made by God to Abraham, whether through the medium of vision or by some direct communication.

First, there was the promise of the *land*. When the patriarch arrived in Shechem, in the plain of Moreh, the Lord appeared to him and said, "Unto thee will I give this land." The boundaries were set forth in a covenant made some twenty years later, when Abraham was ninety-five, as extending from the river of Egypt (Wady el Arish) in the south-west to the great River Euphrates in the north-east. Some four or five hundred years later Abraham's family, now grown into a nation, found themselves at the entrance of this land (Deut. **1**. 7, 8 and **11**. 24), and they were instructed to read the Law in the plain of Moreh, the very place where Abraham had seen his first vision in Canaan (Deut. **11**. 30). In another five centuries we come to the time of Solomon; and he actually reigned over the land thus described (see 1 Kings **4**. 21, 24). Many a time afterwards the land was invaded and desolated and depopulated; and now in this 20th century after Christ the descendants of Abraham have only a small and perilous footing in it. This little land,

The land.

however, has played a great part in the world's history, and perhaps it will yet be the scene of wonderful events.

The multitudinous seed.

Secondly, there was the promise of numerous *offspring*. The family of Abraham were to become as the stars of heaven for multitude, and as the sand which is on the sea-shore (Gen. **22**. 17). Five hundred years later we find this promise fulfilled (Deut. **1**. 10 ; **10**. 22), the fighting men of Israel being then 600,000. Again, in Solomon's time (1 Kings **4**. 20) the people were as the sand of the sea. They had indeed become a company of peoples (Gen. **35**. 11 ; **48**. 4), and Abraham had become a father of many nations. There are now about ten million of his descendants in the world, scattered among the other nations, and there are no signs of the people dying out. Some 50,000 of them are now in Jerusalem, whereas in 1860 there were only about 7,000 there.

The blessing of all nations.

Thirdly, there was a promise that in one of Abraham's seed *all nations of the earth should be blessed* (Gen. **12**. 3 ; **22**. 18). This remarkable promise was passed on, with the other two, to Isaac and Jacob, and the fulfilment of it must be looked for somewhere within the families of the Twelve Tribes. But we search the Old Testament in vain to find anyone becoming a blessing to the world at large. The Psalms and the Prophets, however, have various references to something which was to be done for the benefit of both Jew and Gentile. Accordingly we turn to the New Testament, and in Acts **3**. 25, 26, we find the old promise brought forth from its resting-place, and the Jews are plainly told that it was fulfilled in Jesus Christ. Comp. also Luke **1**. 55, 70 ; **2**. 32. Moreover, the nature of the blessing which the Lord Jesus bestows on all nations is pointed out by St. Paul. It is primarily the gift of the Holy Spirit, though other blessings were to follow.

PROMISES TO ABRAHAM AND DAVID FULFILLED. 117

Guided by the light thus obtained, we look back to the older Scriptures to enquire whether they contain definite promises concerning the outpouring of the Spirit and the call of the Gentiles.

The action of the Spirit of God on the inner man is an occasional topic in the Old Testament, from Gen. **6**. 3 and onwards, and we learn that the special inspiration of the Spirit was exhibited not only in the prophet, but also in the artificer, the warrior, and the singer. But as the third great promise made to Abraham was to include some special gift or manifestation of the Spirit, who would on this account be called "the Spirit of promise" (Luke **24**. 49; John **15**. 26; Acts **1**. 4; Eph. **1**. 13), we should naturally expect to find some prophetic intimation of it in the Hebrew Scriptures.

The gift of the Spirit.

Turning to Isai. **32**. 15 we find that the outpouring of the Spirit is spoken of in this Messianic chapter as the first step to the reign of righteousness. In Isai. **44**. 3 we read, "I will pour water upon him who is thirsty, and floods upon the dry ground; I will pour My Spirit on thy seed and My blessing on thine offspring." Here we have the promised blessing identified with the gift of the Spirit; and we are forcibly reminded of the invitation of the Lord Jesus to the thirsty soul, and of St. John's comment thereon (John **7**. 37–39). Again, in Isai. **59**. 19–21 there is the promise of the Spirit in connexion with the new covenant; whilst in chap. **61**. 1 we get the true Messianic idea, viz. the anointing of the Divine Messiah or Servant, not with literal oil, but with the Holy Ghost; and then follows an enumeration of the blessings which should flow from Him both on Jew and Gentile. Compare Acts **10**. 38, where St. Peter says that "God anointed the Lord Jesus with the Holy Ghost and with power, and that He went about doing good, and healing all that were oppressed of the devil; for God was with Him." Our Lord's mighty and loving works were thus testimonies to the fact that He was really the Lord's Anointed; and in consequence of this He is commissioned to pass on "the anointing" to His followers (1 John **2.** 27), and to baptize them with the Holy Ghost.

To these passages from Isaiah we should add the notable one in Joel **2.** 28, etc., which St. Peter quoted and applied in his first speech, where he says that the Lord Jesus, having been filled and anointed with the Holy Ghost, "shed forth the Spirit" upon those who believed in Him (Acts **2.** 33). This was the long promised blessing. This was what John the Baptist had spoken of so often, and what the Lord Jesus had announced so plainly in St. Luke **24**, St. John **14**, and Acts **1**. On carefully examining the passage in Joel, we find that the promise was to be fulfilled between the time of the people's repentance and the time of the coming of the great and terrible day of the Lord. The three thousand who repented and were baptized on the Day of Pentecost doubtless obtained the blessing—not necessarily the outward sign, but the inward reality, the indwelling of the Spirit of Christ—and became the first inheritors of the promise; but the expression "all flesh," which occurs in this promise of the outpouring of the Holy Spirit, seems to be world-wide; that is to say, it includes Gentiles as well as Jews; those that were afar off as well as those that were near. Certainly it is generally used in this large sense; comp. Gen. **6.** 12, 13; Num. **16.** 22; Ps. **65.** 2; Isai. **40.** 5, 6; Jer. **32.** 27; and other passages. It is thus parallel with the words in the original promise concerning "all the families of the earth," who were to be blessed in the seed of Abraham. The inclusion of the Gentiles in the blessings to be brought by the Messiah is frequently referred to in the Old Testament. The word גוים, translated "Heathen," "Gentiles," or "Nations," gradually assumed a

The Gentiles.

technical sense in the days of Moses; and in Deut. **32.** 43 the Song of Israel closes with the prospect of blessing, not for the Jew only, but also for the Gentile. This is one of the passages singled out by St. Paul (Rom. **15.** 9, 10) as indicating that the promises in Christ were for the Gentiles. The thought is taken up by David in Ps. **18.** 49 (2 Sam. **22.** 50), and in other Psalms (see Pss. **47.** 8 ; **67.** 2 ; **72.** 11 ; **86.** 9).

Isaiah frequently refers to this bright prospect and introduces it into Messianic prophecies ; see, *e.g.* Isai. **2.** 2, where " all nations " are spoken of as sharing Israel's blessings; chap. **11.** 10, where the Gentiles flock to the standard of the Son of Jesse ; **42.** 1, 6, where the Messiah brings forth judgment to the Gentiles ; **49.** 6, where Christ is a light to lighten the Gentiles (comp. Luke **2.** 32 and Acts **13.** 47). Similarly, the later prophets, Zechariah and Malachi, speak of the Messiah as speaking peace to the Gentiles (Zech. **9.** 10), and of God's name being great among them (Mal. **1.** 11). A careful study of the passages in Isaiah points to the truth that the Gentiles would be associated with Israel in a special sense in the days of the Messiah. There would be a Jewish or Israelite nucleus and Gentile adherents, or, as St. Paul puts it, an Israelite tree and Gentile grafts.

In the New Testament this subject is only occasionally spoken of during our Lord's lifetime, *e.g.* in Matt. **8.** 11 and **21.** 43. But our Lord's post-resurrection commission to preach and testify to all the nations was gradually understood and acted upon, first by St. Peter and subsequently by St. Paul; and it is to St. Paul that we owe it, under God, that Christianity, instead of being the religion of a Jewish sect, became a world-wide faith, so that in this last past century—to take the latest and brightest example—the Gospel has been preached to nations speaking four hundred languages and covering a very large portion of the world. Thus it is

The Messiah.

that the blessing promised to Abraham is being wrought out in Christendom under our very eyes, and, it may be, in our own experience.

We now come to a fourth promise, made many centuries after the time of Abraham, though indicated by Jacob in his parting blessing (see *supra*, chap. XIII.). David is now the Messiah, the anointed of the Lord. As such he fights Israel's battles, conquers their enemies, and organises their kingdom. In addition to his other labours he desires to build a permanent Temple in place of the Tabernacle; but a message comes to him from God, saying, that the honour of building a Temple is not for him but for his son. Then a promise is added which fills David's heart with wonder. In was that his kingly dynasty was to be permanent. In spite of all their failures and defects God would never take away His mercy from the line of David (2 Sam. 7; 1 Chron. 17). According to this promise we trace the dynasty of David up to the Captivity and on to the Restoration—though the kingdom, as such, was never restored. Then the Old Testament fails us, but the New Testament gives two genealogies which lead on to Joseph, who is called the son of David (Matt. 1. 20; Luke 1. 27), and into whose family Jesus, the Son of the Virgin Mary,[*] was adopted. In this wonderful way God "raised up seed" to David (Luke 1. 69). Every pious Jew must have expected that the Messiah would come, and Israel had been waiting for a king for five centuries, since the time of Zorobabel.

---

[*] It has been pointed out in a previous chapter that though it is not definitely stated that Mary was of the tribe of Judah, it was more than probable that she was. Her child was to sit on the throne of David His father, and of His kingdom there was to be no end (Luke 1. 32). The two genealogies are manifestly Joseph's; and if the crown of David had been put on any head it might have legitimately come to Joseph. Jesus was Joseph's son by adoption (formally or informally) and Mary's son by Divine Grace. Mary's father may have been akin to Joseph and her mother to Elizabeth.

PROMISES TO ABRAHAM AND DAVID FULFILLED. 121

At last He had come, having been "born King of the Jews." Meanwhile, the Messianic idea, which was simple enough at the outset, had been widened and deepened in consequence of a series of prophetic utterances during the three great prophetic periods. In the first, Hosea had declared that David (*i.e.* the Son of David, see *supra*, chap. XI.) would be the bond of union among the Tribes; Amos had said that David's tent, which had fallen down, should be set up again; Micah had promised that the remnant of Israel should become a strong people, and the Lord should reign over them; he had also pointed to Beth-lehem as the birthplace of the Son of David; and Isaiah had spoken of the virgin-born Child who should occupy David's throne for ever, and should be a root of Jesse to whom the Gentiles should come. In the second great prophetic period the days were degenerate, and the Books abound in serious warnings and exhortations, but promises are not lacking. Jeremiah and Ezekiel point to the re-establishment of the kingdom under one Shepherd and King, who should be David (*i.e.* the Son of David); and Daniel tells wonderful things concerning the Son of Man Who should become Ruler over the nations. Then come the later prophets, Haggai and Zechariah, who speak of One who was destined to be the great Temple-builder, and in that sense a true Son of David.

All these and many other passages point to a coming King, raised up into the family of David, ruling over the house of Jacob, and supreme over the nations. This is the Messianic idea. But, guided by the light of the New Testament, we find that another idea had to be combined with it. In order to see what this was we must step back a little. Israel was always taught that God was the true King of men, ruling them, judging them, saving them. But God had been rejected, and the people had determined to have an earthly king such as the surrounding nations possessed. Saul, the tallest and finest of men, was selected; and after him David was selected, though he had neither stature nor position to boast of. The anointing of the kings marked that God delegated His authority to them, but reminded them that they were to use that authority for Him and not for themselves. But the kings failed. Even the best of them—Hezekiah and Josiah—did not bring men's hearts back to God. The Divine supremacy must therefore be re-asserted in some way which would win men back to their true allegiance. How could his be done?

Spiritual side of the promise.

All the way through human history there had been a great need. The Law of Moses had not created it, but had intensified it, though unable to relieve it. The system of atoning sacrifice and priest gave no satisfaction to the conscience, but it pointed upward to God's willingness to forgive, and forward to some possibility in the future. What should be done? Supposing that sacrificial feast and burnt-offering and meat-offering and sin-offering were done away, could something better take their place, and could some One better take the place of the priest? It is here that such passages as we have in the 40th and 110th Psalms come in, also the 53rd of Isaiah. They seem to answer to the desire of the human conscience—"If only One would come from heaven and do something for us and in us which would make us good and acceptable to God, then we should fear no evil." Perhaps no one ever put the thought into such words as these, but God, who recognised human needs better than man himself knew them, has answered the mute sighing of the world.

Accordingly, we find that the Messianic idea gradually combines itself with, and to some extent and for a time becomes subordinate to, the sacrificial one. In the Gospels we learn of One who comes from heaven to do His Father's

PROMISES TO ABRAHAM AND DAVID FULFILLED. 123

will, and who suffers all the indignities which human sin can devise, bearing them because they represented to Him the world's failure to do right, and tasting the death which is the natural outcome of evil. Then He rises supreme over corruption, the grave, and earth itself, and sits on the throne of God awaiting the day of a glorious manifestation of the Divine sovereignity and supremacy founded upon love.

This view of the Divine purpose was only dimly adumbrated in the Old Testament, and the Lord Jesus barely refers to it in His teaching; but when once men had come to believe in Jesus as the person marked out to be the King of men, the sacrificial side of His work was freely taught, as we see from the writings of St. Peter, St. John, and St. Paul. This, in fact, became the most notable element in that Gospel of Peace which was the power of God unto salvation.

This then is the Divine order. First the King is revealed; then He poured out His soul unto death and bare the sins of many; then He blesses men with His Holy Spirit, whilst His ministers proclaim His message to the world. Meanwhile He is building up His Temple, which is made of spiritual stones, Jewish and Gentile; and the gates of Hades shall not prevail against the community which He is constructing. The everlasting Kingdom of God is thus being established under a Divine Priest-King to whom all judgment is delegated. In this way the political aspect of the Mission of Christ gives way to the spiritual, the Jewish to the world-wide, the seen and temporal to the unseen and eternal. Then will come the final triumph.

The Old Testament programme concerning the Messiah is fragmentary. It is like a puzzle-map of which the pieces are discovered in Books written in many different centuries and under varied circumstances. But Jesus appears in the fulness of time. Little by little His adherents begin to put some of the pieces together and find them fulfilled in Him. Still something was wanting. He died, and all seemed confusion again; but shortly afterwards He Himself expounded the Scriptures concerning Himself, pointing out that the Law, the Prophets, and the Psalms testified to the fact that He must first suffer and afterwards be glorified. Then all became clear. But it will be clearer still hereafter when men's eyes shall behold the King in His Beauty and Glory, exercising functions compared with which all that we associate with the idea of kingship will seem as nothing.

CHAPTER XVI.

THE TEN TRIBES.

IN spite of occasional jealousies and contentions the Tribes or Clans of which Israel was composed held fairly together until the end of Solomon's reign. But in the age of Rehoboam and Jeroboam the kingdom was split into two. Henceforth we read of two Houses (Isai. **8**. 14), two Families (Jer. **33**. 24), two Nations (Ezek. **35**. 10). The one of these is ordinarily called Judah, and with it there was amalgamated the whole of the Tribe of Benjamin, the greater part of Simeon, and a considerable portion of Levi, including the House of Aaron. The other is called Israel, or Ephraim, or the House of Joseph. The metropolis of the one was Jerusalem or Zion, and of the other Samaria. From Jeroboam's time onward the word Israel is used in two senses, standing either for the Twelve Tribes or for the Northern Kingdom. Up to the time of the Captivity of the Ten Tribes the word is generally used in the latter sense, though not always. It appears that the kindred expression "House of Jacob" stands generally for the Twelve Tribes as a whole, and frequently as if represented in Jerusalem (see Mic. **3**. 9; Obad. 17; Isai. **58**. 1). *Two uses of the word "Israel."*

There were two stages of the captivity of the Northern Kingdom, which are represented in the following passages:— *Captivity of the Ten Tribes.*

i. "In the days of Pekah king of Israel, Tiglath-pileser king of Assyria came and took Ijon and Abel-beth-maachah and Janoah and Kedesh and Hazor and Gilead and Galilee, all the land of Naphtali, and carried them captive to Assyria" (2 Kings **15**. 29). It will be observed that this deportation affected the north and east, and left Samaria itself untouched. There is a reference to it in Isai. **9.** 1 (see R.V.).

ii. " Shalmaneser king of Assyria came up against Hoshea, and Hoshea became his servant and gave him presents." Subsequently the king of Assyria shut him up and bound him in prison; "and the king of Assyria came up throughout all the land and went up to Samaria and besieged it three years. In the ninth year of Hoshea, the king of Assyria (Sargon) took Samaria and carried Israel away into Assyria and placed them in Halah and in Habor (by) the river of Gozan and in the cities of the Medes " (2 Kings **17.** 3-6). In a further account of the later captivity (2 Kings **18.** 10, 11, 12) the words used are exactly the same; and the reason for the affliction is given in a condensed form, viz., " Because they obeyed not the voice of the Lord their God, but transgressed His covenant and all that Moses the servant of the Lord commanded," a passage which shows that the Northern Tribes ought to have regarded themselves as still under the Mosaic covenant.

At first sight we might suppose that the Ten Tribes were now blotted out, with the exception of those who were deported into the Median cities, and whom it is the fashion to describe as "lost." But this can hardly have been the case. Whilst "Samaria and its cities" were now largely occupied by foreigners (2 Kings **17.** 24), including Babylonians, there must have been a considerable *residuum* of Israelites in the land.

The saved Remnant.

It was not entirely depopulated, as is clearly shown from what took place in the days of Josiah. This godly and zealous king considered it his duty to purge the cities of Samaria as well as the Judean cities, following therein the example of Hezekiah, and seeking spiritual, if not political, reunion as Hezekiah had done (see 2 Chron. **30** and **31**). Accordingly he purged the cities of Manasseh and Ephraim and Simeon even unto Naphtali, and cut down all the idols throughout all the land of Israel (2 Chron. **34.** 6, 7). In his eighteenth year there was a great collection of offerings from Manasseh and Ephraim "*and all the Remnant of Israel*" (chap. **34.** 9), as well as from Judah and Benjamin. This passage shows us that all the Tribes were regarded as having an interest in the repair of the Temple. We are told, further, that Josiah took away all the abominations out of all the countries that pertained to the children of Israel and made all that were present in Israel to serve the Lord (chap. **34.** 33). And all were instructed by the Levites and were united in keeping the Passover (chap. **35.** 2, 18).

It must not be forgotten, moreover, that at the beginning of the kingdom there was a nucleus of most, if not all, the Tribes under David's special leadership (1 Chron. **12**), and that Jerusalem, having been metropolis of all the Tribes before the secession, would probably be a refuge and rallying-place through the period that followed (see 2 Chron. **23.** 2 ; **24.** 5, 16 ; **28.** 23).

Turning to the prophecies, we may lay it down as a general rule that wherever Judah and Israel are contrasted (as in Hosea **1.** 6, 11 ; **4.** 15 ; Amos **2.** 4, 6), the latter title refers to the Northern Kingdom ; but that wherever "Israel" is seen to be parallel with "the House of Jacob," the reference would be to the Twelve Tribes, who were evidently regarded as conserved and represented in the land in spite of the great deportation to Media. So it came to pass that the Southern Kingdom, after the fourth year of Hezekiah, was not only part of Israel, but represented the interests of Israel as a whole, and that prophecies concerning "Israel" would then be naturally understood as referring to the "Remnant," whose head quarters would be Jerusalem, though they might be found also in sadly diminished numbers scattered throughout all parts of the land.

In accordance with this view we read that "*all Israel* were carried to Babylon" (1 Chron. 9. 1), and that apparently on their return there dwelt in Jerusalem not only children of Judah and Benjamin, but of Ephraim and Manasseh (*v.* 2), and that *the Remnant of Israel* were in all the cities of Judah (Neh. 11. 20). This explains the offering of twelve bullocks and twelve he-goats for all Israel (Ezra 8. 35 ; comp. chap. 6. 17–21 ; 7. 10 ; 9. 1 ; 10. 5, 23). It has been estimated that at least a quarter of those who returned from captivity were of the Ten Tribes. Whether this view be accepted or not, there cannot be any reasonable doubt that from the time of the Restoration until the final fall of Jerusalem, at the hand of the Romans, all the Tribes were regarded as represented in the land of Israel, though many families of all the Tribes were also to be found in the neighbouring countries. (See Acts 2. 7–11).

The conclusion to be arrived at is that as a *Kingdom* the Ten Tribes were done away with, but some of them remained as part of the original stock of Israel and Jacob ; they were thus included in "the Remnant of Jacob" at the time of the Restoration ; even then they had one Head (Zerubbabel), and the two sticks were once more one (see Ezek. 37).*

Prophecies concerning the Remnant.

The general course of events thus indicated had been a matter of prediction as far back as the time of Moses. See Lev. 26 and Deut. 27—29. The prophets of the age of Hezekiah are full and free in their utterances concerning the impending doom of the Northern Kingdom as such in contrast with the Southern. "I will no more have mercy on the House of Israel, but I will utterly (*i.e.* surely) take them away ; but I will have mercy on the House of Judah and will save them" (Hos. 1. 6, 7). Yet God is loth to give them up, and urges

---

* Since these pages were written I have seen Mr. David Barron's *The Ancient Scripture and the Modern Jew*, in which the same line is taken as against the theory that the Ten Tribes were "lost."

them ere it is too late to seek Him. "How shall I give thee
up, Ephraim? How shall I deliver thee, Israel?" (Hos. **11.** 8).
"Thus saith the Lord unto the House of Israel, seek ye Me and
ye shall live" (Amos **5.** 4). God would not lightly cast away any
of the Twelve Tribes. In spite of all their sins Isaiah and
Hosea announced that a Remnant should return. The children
of Judah and the children of Israel should be gathered together
and appoint themselves one Head and shall come up out of the
land, *i.e.* out of the land of captivity (Hos. **1.** 11). The children of Israel should return and seek the Lord their God
(*i.e.* shall seek Him once again) and David their king; and
should fear the Lord and His goodness in the latter days
(Hos. **3.** 5). The Tribes as represented by these remnants
would thus be amalgamated. When the captivity of treacherous
Judah and Jerusalem, including the backsliding Israelite remnant, was impending, the Lord still besought them to return;
and Jeremiah took up the touching words of Hos. **14.** 4: "I
will heal your backslidings." This call was to go to the North,
i.e. to the most distant regions of the Captivity; and the promise was made that if they did return to God, even though it
were only one of a city or two of a family, He on His part
would bring them back to Zion (Jerusalem being regarded as
their headquarters), "and in those days the House of Judah
shall walk with * the House of Israel, and they shall come
together out of the land of the north to the land which I have
given for an inheritance unto your fathers" (Jer. **3.** 6–22).

Still, however, the promise stood and was reiterated. "I *The Twelve Tribes re-*
will bring again the captivity of Israel and Judah. I will *united.*
cause them to return. . . . It is the time of Jacob's

---

* In the margin (A.V. and R.V.) we read "to" for "with"; but see Exod. 35. 22, where the same Hebrew preposition (ל) is used,—"Both men and women" lit. "men to women"; similarly, the text above might be translated "Both the House of Judah and the House of Israel."

trouble, but he shall be saved out of it. . . . They shall serve the Lord their God and David their king, whom I will raise up unto them" (Jer. **30.** 1-9). Thus the promise made through Hosea is taken up and pressed home by Jeremiah: it affects both the Israelite and the Judean remnant, and reunion is definitely promised. "The watchmen on mount Ephraim shall cry, Arise, and let us go up to Zion unto the Lord our God . . . . for I am a father to Israel, and Ephraim is My firstborn. . . . They shall come and sing in the height of Zion. . . . Israel and Judah shall be re-sown, and the new covenant shall be established with the two Houses, and the seed of Israel shall never be cast off" (Jer. **31**; comp. chap. **33**). This reunion and return is timed in chap. **50.** 4 as contemporary with the downfall of Babylon. "In those days and in that time the children of Israel shall come, they and the children of Judah together, going and weeping, they shall go and seek the Lord their God. They shall ask the way to Zion with their faces thitherward, saying, Come and let us join ourselves to the Lord in an everlasting covenant that shall not be forgotten" (Jer. **50.** 4, 5; comp. chap. **51.** 5).

The re-union accomplished. From these utterances it is clear that the Remnant of the two Houses which had been taken to Babylon and the north, both Judean and Israelite, was to return under one head, who should be a representative of the House of David. This promise was fulfilled in a measure when the people returned under Zerubbabel, and when Zion became, as we have seen, the centre of worship to representatives of all the Tribes, though the Remnant that returned was sadly small.

Ezekiel, Jeremiah's contemporary, prophesies to the same effect. After convicting "the shepherds of Israel" of shameful neglect, God promises to bring the lost sheep back to their own mountains and to set up one Shepherd over them, even "My servant David." "He shall feed them and shall be thei

Shepherd" (chap. **34**. 23). The whole House of Israel is to be brought forth as if from the grave, to be breathed upon by God's Spirit, and the two branches of the children of Israel are to be made one, under one king, and not to be two kingdoms any more, "and David My servant shall be king over them," and God would make an everlasting covenant with them (chap. **37**). Again, in the closing vision of the Book, all the Tribes have their share in the land, Joseph having two portions as before (chap. **47**. 13).

One has to keep reminding oneself that these prophecies of Jeremiah and Ezekiel were uttered before the seventy years' Captivity was completed, and that the Return under Zerubbabel was the first fulfilment. This was "the foreground," at any rate, though there is a Messianic background.

The ambiguity of the word "Israel" has led to much discussion concerning the so-called "lost Tribes." But none of the Tribes were "lost" in the sense in which this expression is generally used, though all of them were "lost" in another sense; see Matt. **10**. 6. The Israel of the magnificent prophecies of Isaiah is the amalgamated Remnant which, and which alone, from his time onwards, represented all the Twelve Tribes.* Some of them returned in the days of Zorobabel, Ezra, and Nehemiah, and some remained in the far East. Later dispersions from the centre followed, but all were one Body, as in the days of the Lord and His Apostles (see Luke **22**. 30; Acts **26**. 7; James **1**. 1).

The distinction between the Ten Tribes and the Two is non-existent in the New Testament. As both sets of Tribes were under the Old Covenant, so both were invited to share in the blessings of the New (see Jer. **31**. 31–34, compared with

---

* In Ezekiel (chaps. 8, 9, 11—14, 18—22) the House of Israel is regarded as still centred at Jerusalem, but destined to go into captivity in Babylon.

Heb. **8.** 8-12). Judah is included in Israel in some passages, and Israel in Judah in others.* The two are one, and the middle wall of partition which existed between them from the days of Rehoboam till the days of Hoshea exists no more.

Nothing is more clear than that as Israel was originally one family, so they were to become one again. The only serious questions are these: Have the numerous prophecies uttered before the return from Babylon been fulfilled? Did the common disaster and the common hope blend the Tribes into one? Did one ruler lead back the representative remnant of all the Tribes when Cyrus issued his edict? and did those who failed to return keep more or less in touch with their more loyal brethren so as to be one nation, though dispersed? The passages referred to above seem to give an unqualified affirmative in reply to these questions. As Zion was the headquarters of the representative remnant before the Captivity, so it was afterwards. In this sense only can we understand the prediction in the Book of Joel, that the prosperity of *Zion* is the guarantee that God is in the midst of *Israel* (chap. **2.** 27). In this sense we understand the return of "the remnant of Jacob," which is promised as an encouragement to Zion in Isai. **10.** 20-24. In this sense we understand the blended references to Zion and Israel in the second portion of Isaiah (chaps. **40—66**); comp. also Zeph. **3.** 13-15. This representative remnant, perhaps at a later stage of its existence, is spoken of in Zech. **8.** 13, where we read, "As ye were a curse among the heathen, O House of Judah and House of Israel, so will I save you, and ye shall be a blessing."

---

* Probably long before New Testament times the word "Jew" was used not for men of the Tribe of Judah only, but for Israel as a whole. See Esth. 8. 9, which speaks of the "Jews" as to be found from India to Ethiopia. The word was then what the word "Hebrew" was in far more ancient days.

THE TEN TRIBES.

Comparatively few prophetic passages have to do with the subsequent history of those of the Ten Tribes who were deported by the Assyrians. The apocryphal passage 2 Esdras 13. 40 is of no authority. The God of Israel preserved the Remnant in the way above detailed, and that was enough. Many passages which speak of Judah speak of it as containing the nucleus of all the Tribes. The blessings connected with the return from Captivity were for the godly and willing remnant of all the Tribes. All, doubtless, were represented when Christ and His followers went among "the lost sheep of the house of Israel," and when the Spirit descended on the Day of Pentecost. The New Covenant was for all, and the outpouring of the Spirit was not restricted in any way. There seems, therefore, to be neither room nor necessity for that view of "the lost sheep of the house of Israel" which lies at the basis of the Anglo-Israel theory.

At the same time it is quite within the bounds of possibility that representatives of the Northern Kingdom may have lived on for centuries in the far East, broken away from the true Remnant and yet not amalgamated with other nations. The existence of the Falashas in Abyssinia, the Afghan tradition, the relics of Khae-fung-foo, and the travellers' tales concerning the Beni-Rediab make such a view quite reasonable.

CHAPTER XVII.

ISRAEL'S FUTURE.

Unfulfilled Prophecy.

THE prophecies which we have been briefly considering in the last two chapters take us from the age of Abraham —some 2,000 years B.C.—to the time when the Lord Jesus came to earth. His birth, ministry, death, resurrection, and ascension, together with the outpouring of the Spirit, are the fulfilment of a long series of Old Testament predictions. The evidence is cumulative. We are not dealing with a few isolated vaticinations, but with a long series, definite in expression and preparatory for the greatest event in human history. We naturally ask ourselves, as we take a further survey of the Books, Is all that has been predicted now accomplished? or is there a *residuum* of unfulfilled prophecy standing over for accomplishment in the future? It is clear in the first place, when we examine our materials, that there remain certain unfulfilled sections in the Old Testament; and that portions of the prophetic teaching of the Lord Himself and of the Apostles have to do with the time of the end, to which we are drawing nearer century by century. Secondly, as to the events predicted which were still future during the lifetime of Christ, there were announced the fall of Jerusalem and the consequent dispersion of Israel, the evangelisation of the world, the development of false teaching and persecution, the restoration of Israel, the final break-up of the world-empires, the first resurrection, the manifestation of Christ in

ISRAEL'S FUTURE.

His glorious kingdom, the judgment of quick and dead, and the establishment of new heavens and a new earth.

The mere enumeration of these subjects is impressive; they are grand in themselves, and they present ideas which are of the deepest interest to the race and to the individual. In dealing with them it seems best to secure some outline analogous with that contained in the Song of Israel (Deut. **32**),* if such a one is to be found. An outline of a very comprehensive and far-reaching character has been preserved to us in the first three Gospels as it fell from the lips of our Lord Himself; and all other New Testament utterances arrange themselves more or less clearly in connexion with it. *Our Lord's outline.*

When we compare the 24th of St. Matthew with the 13th of St. Mark and the 21st of St. Luke, we find presented to us three accounts of one discourse relating to a series of events, some of which were in the immediate future. The best commentary on the greater part of the discourse is furnished unwittingly by Josephus in his *Book of the Wars*. The Temple furnishes the text. In spite of its beauty and magnificence, the Lord told His followers that it was to be thrown down. Struck by this amazing announcement the four fishermen afterwards made private enquiries concerning the details. They wanted to know three things: (i.) When the overthrow should take place? (ii.) What should be the sign of Christ's coming?† and (iii.) What should be the sign of the final consummation? Evidently there is a great deal involved in these questions. Perhaps the second sprang out of the first, whilst the third arose out of our Lord's teaching by parables, especially those recorded in Matt. **13**. If we could picture up what was in the mind of the enquirers

---

* See *supra*, chap. II. § 4.
† It is remarkable that the word for "*coming*" ($\pi\alpha\rho o\upsilon\sigma\iota\alpha$) which is used by St. Matthew never occurs again till the Epistles.

at this stage, perhaps we should conclude that the Lord's coming was for the purpose of destroying the Temple and for the ushering in of the new and glorious Dispensation which would be inaugurated at the completion of the old one, when the Kingdom would be restored to Israel (Acts 1. 6).

Our Lord's answer contains various parts. They may be shortly exhibited thus :—

i. Do not be led astray by pretended Messiahs.

ii. Do not be disturbed by rumours of wars.

iii. Prepare to be hated and persecuted.

iv. Exercise endurance amid the temptation to apostatise.

v. The Gospel shall be preached through the (Roman?) world before the end (see note p. 140).

vi. At last the time will come. The first symptom will be the sight of "the Abomination of Desolation standing in the holy place" (Matthew); "where it ought not" (Mark); or as it is paraphrased in St. Luke, "Jerusalem compassed with armies." The desolation would then be at hand.

vii. Take flight at once. "For these are the days of retribution, that all things which are written may be fulfilled"(Luke).

viii. The distress that follows will be intense, but it will be shortened for the sake of the Chosen People (Matthew and Mark).

ix. Many of the people shall be slain; others led captive to all nations; Jerusalem shall be trodden down by the Gentiles until the times of the Gentiles be fulfilled (Luke).

x. Beware during this period, as during the earlier one, of being led astray by false Christs, for the real *Parousia*, or coming of the Son of Man, will be very different from any local rising.

xi. At length, when all the tribulation and down-treading is measured out and the times of the Gentiles are thus fulfilled, there will be signs in heaven and catastrophes on earth. The sign of the Son of Man shall be seen in heaven and the

Tribes shall mourn, and men shall see Him coming in (or *on*) the clouds of heaven with power and great glory.

xii. Then the redemption of the people draws nigh; and God will gather together His chosen ones from all places where they have been scattered.

The main body of the prophetic discourse is now complete; and one cannot fail to be struck with the calmness and clearness of the announcement and with the dignity of Him who thus deliberately draws aside the veil from the future. The prediction naturally falls into certain groups or portions, thus:—§§ i.–v. are preliminary; §§ vi.–ix. describe the fall of Jerusalem; §§ x.–xii. describe what is to follow when the times of the Gentiles are fulfilled,—so that it is only these last that can refer to what is still future. The short parable of the fig-tree that follows encourages the Lord's followers to look out for certain symptoms probably at each stage. The fulfilment of the first group would guarantee the fulfilment of the second, and that (which is now far in the past) encourages us to believe in the fulfilment of the third. The first and second groups were fulfilled in the lifetime of men of that generation. Even the preaching to the Roman world was regarded as an accomplished fact in St. Paul's time. See Rom. **10.** 18; Col. **1.** 6, 23. The third group shall also be fulfilled in its time, though many generations of men have passed away since our Lord's utterance. The exact date of this, *i.e.* the *Parousia* and the Restitution of Israel, was not revealed even to the Lord Jesus Himself,—and it is to be noticed that this was the only event which the Son was not in a position to reveal. All the rest lay before Him like an open record; but this point of time the Father had kept under His own control (see Acts **1.** 7). It will be sudden, however, and the Lord will come like a thief in the night, and will finally separate those who have been employed together in the ordinary avocations of life, some being taken * and others left behind.

The discourse closes with an exhortation to watch and to be faithful in service. It is followed in St. Matthew by the series of parabolic discourses contained in the 25th chapter, which are intended to illustrate the destiny of the various groups of persons who will find themselves brought into contact with the Lord at the time of the end.

The outline presented in this discourse appears to be mainly Israelite in its bearing; and this would be as much as the Apostles could receive at that time. The "elect" all through appear to be the chosen people, the remnant of the House of Jacob, not the Christian Church. The tribes who lament appear to be the Israelite tribes. The gathering of the people from all regions seems to be the Restitution so often predicted in the Old Testament, and it ushers in the time when the true Messiah shall reign over Israel. Thus the framework of the prophecy appears to be Israelite. Much, however, is left to be filled up, especially with regard to the times of the Gentiles; and this can be done in a measure in the light of the Lord's parables and of the Apostles' teaching, a careful study of which makes it clear that there is another side to the *Parousia* to be read along with this Messianic and Israelite side.

Israel's prospects.

That Israel has a great future is clear from Scripture as a whole. There is a large unfulfilled element in the Old Testament which demands it, unless we spiritualise it away or relinquish it as Oriental hyperbole. This scattered nation of ten million people has yet its part to play in the history of the world. There is to be a re-betrothal, a reunion, a liberation, a conversion, a restoration, which shall be like a resurrection,

---

* Compare John 14. 3, "I will take you to Myself," where the same Greek word is used.

or life from the dead. There will be a time of prosperity, an entrance into the New Covenant, with new responsibilities and enlarged influence. All this may be preceded by worse troubles than any which have befallen Israel hitherto; but the texts which are supposed to imply this may have been already fulfilled since they were uttered.

The great condition of Restitution (according to St. Peter's preaching) is that Israel, as a people, should repent and turn to the Lord. Then will come the times of refreshing (Acts 3. 19-21). Similarly, St. Paul says that a veil is on Israel's mind, but that when the people shall turn to the Lord the veil shall be taken away (2 Cor. 3. 16). In the Epistle to the Romans (chaps. 9—11) he goes fully into the matter, and shows that the children of the Kingdom are cast out through unbelief. They are rejected because they have rejected God. This hardness of Israel's heart and lot has been permitted, and, in that sense, ordered, first, so that they might carry out the predetermined crucifixion of Christ, and secondly, that the Gentiles might have the predestined opportunity of receiving the Truth. When, however, " the fulness of the Gentiles has come in " (or, to use our Lord's words, when " the times of the Gentiles are fulfilled ") then Israel, as a people, will be " saved," and will enter into the New Covenant. See especially Rom. 11. 25, 26. They are still God's chosen people, and His gifts and calling are " without repentance," *i.e.* are irreversible. As long as the world goes on Israel will be a people. Now they reject Christ; hereafter they will accept Him; a great future is then before them, and they are yet to be a blessing to the nations.

It is difficult to believe that there will be no local centre for the restored people. They will not be a kingdom in the sense in which they were in old times, but they will be a vast community, with organisation and worship and ministration which the Old Testament naturally expresses in terms borrowed from the past. They will not be "Zionists" in the modern sense, but Zion may be yet their true centre.

So far the Nationalist view of our Lord's prophecy concerning His *Parousia* has been touched upon; but the Epistles graft upon it a Christian view, and to this we must now address ourselves.

Note on Matthew 24. 14.

"This Gospel of the Kingdom shall be proclaimed in all the world for a witness to all nations; and then shall come the end." St. Mark puts it shortly, "The Gospel must first be proclaimed to all nations." The word translated "world" (οἰκουμένη) is sometimes equivalent to the Roman Empire (see Luke 2. 1 and Acts 11. 28), but is not rigidly confined to this sense. In Matt. 26. 13, where we have another reference to the Gospel being preached in all the world, the wider word (*Kosmos*) is used. The preaching to "all nations" seems to be unrestricted in chap. 28. 19 and Mark 16. 15. No wider words could be used. Shall we take the text before us in the restricted or in the unrestricted sense? Alford's note on its runs thus:—"The Gospel was preached throughout the whole 'orbis terrarum,' and every nation received its testimony before the destruction of Jerusalem; see Col. 1. 6, 23; 2 Tim. 4. 17. This was necessary not only as regarded the Gentiles, but to give to God's people, the few who were scattered among all these nations, the opportunity of receiving or rejecting the preaching of Christ. But in the wider sense the words imply that the Gospel shall be preached in all the world, literally taken, before the great and final end come. The apostacy of the latter days and the universal dispersion of missions are the two great signs of the end drawing near." Thus, behind the Jewish foreground there is a world-wide background in this remarkable discourse.

CHAPTER XVIII.

THE PAROUSIA AND THE MILLENNIUM.

WE gather from our Lord's great prophetic discourse that the day of His appearing or coming is to follow more or less speedily after the completion of "the times of the Gentiles." This *Parousia* naturally assumed great prominence in the minds of the Apostles and of their immediate followers. When we study their writings carefully we are surprised to see how little they say about death and much about the *Parousia* of Christ. The fact of it, rather than the time, is usually dealt with, but it is always regarded as within the possibilities of the near future. In his earliest epistles St. Paul points out that it is to be preceded by the Apostacy, and followed by the Judgment. At times it seemed very near, but obstacles arose, and have arisen again and again, partly spiritual, partly secular or political, partly of the nature of persecutions, which have checked the progress of events, whilst the delay has practically tended to enlarge the boundaries of Christ's Kingdom. The fall of Jerusalem was within ten years of the time of St. Paul's imprisonment, though no one knew it. Probably some expected it (according to the original terms of the decree of Dan. 9) within three years and a half of our Lord's Crucifixion (see *supra*, chap. IV.). Many may have expected the "times of the Gentiles," which began in Apostolic days, to come to an end before the close of the last century, but they are still running on, and no one on earth can tell the day or hour, or even the year, when the signal will be given for the close of the present dispensation and the restitution of Israel.

The hope of the Church.

One thing is clearly elicited from the Epistles: the *Parousia* of the Lord is the hope not only of Israel, but of the Christian Community. It is not only a time of refreshing to Israel, but also a time of the revealing of secrets and of giving rewards and penalties to the Church (1 Cor. **3**. 13-15) ; a time when ministers and converts will stand face to face before each other and before Christ (1 Thess. **2**. 19) ; a time of rest for the troubled (2 Thess. **1**. 7) ; and a time of manifestation of the sons of God (Rom. **8**. 19). But most of all it will be a time of the resurrection of the true saints (1 Cor. **15**. 22), when they shall be metamorphosed and made like their Master, and shall share His glory (Phil. **3**. 20, 21 ; Col. **3**. 4 ; 2 Tim. **2**. 11, 12 ; **4.** 1, 8 ; 1 Pet. **4**. 5 ; 1 John **3**. 2). It is this blessed time, and not the hour of departure, which is looked for throughout the Epistles.

The *Parousia* of Christ is thus invested with tremendous significance. If it means restitution for repentant Israel it means resurrection for "those that are Christ's." Earthly and heavenly glory are thus strangely linked, and the Kingdom of Christ as then manifested will embrace two vast departments of the human race, one of which will have gone through the process of resurrection, and the other will still be in their mortal bodies, the latter being centred in Jerusalem which is below, the former in Jerusalem which is (at present) above.

The human mind, as now constructed, seems incapable of interpreting the passages which will then be fulfilled, or of picturing up the thrilling scenes which are still curtained off from us by futurity, and only seen "through a glass darkly." But putting aside physical speculations, there is one question which may fairly be considered ; it has to do with the continuance of what we may describe as the two-fold kingdom, the Israelite and the saintly. Is the *Parousia* an event, or an epoch ? With regard to Israel the promise was that the Son of David was to reign over it "for ever" (comp. Isai. **9**. 7 with

Luke **1**. 33), and this word "for ever" signifies that as long as the nation existed to be ruled over, so long the Messiah should rule over them.* The resurrection of the saints, on the other hand, points to an event rather than an epoch. It will take place "in the twinkling of an eye at the last trump"; though the judgment or assignment of positions to those who belong to Christ suggests the possibility of an extended period.

It is our business now to consider one of the most notable passages in the New Testament. It may safely be said that if we had not the 20th chapter of Revelation we should know nothing of the *Millennium*. We might indeed read of Jewish ideas of a somewhat similar character, though their date is very uncertain, and we might have guessed from some words of St. Paul and of the Lord Himself that there was a first resurrection from the dead as well as a final resurrection of the dead; and we might have anticipated that the Restitution of Israel would be followed by a time of great blessing on earth; but it is this chapter which gives definiteness to all such anticipations. *The Millennium..*

The early Church seems to have been much attracted by the prospect of the Millennium. Perhaps it took too prominent a position in their minds, so that after the fifth century it was discredited and almost lost sight of until the Reformation. Even if we regard it as altogether figurative, still it prefigures something, for the Seer is very definite in his language and details of what will happen at its close. We naturally associate it with the Restitution which follows upon the *Parousia*, though other interpretations have been suggested. But if this view be correct we must conclude that while the Restitution ushers in a long period of happiness and blessing on earth to the Jew first, and also to the Gentile, there will be

---

* See *Old Testament Synonyms*, chap. 30, on the Hebrew and Greek words which mark duration.

a concurrent reign of certain saints and martyrs with Christ in glory. This latter reign may be supposed to be a time of influence for good (whether upon earth or in the spirit-world) analogous with that now exercised by angels. It will be a true Kingdom of Heaven, in which the meek, the pure, and the persecuted for righteousness sake, will have a share, the way being made more easy through the compulsory withdrawal of the Evil One. There is nothing said about the reign being visible. It is probably spiritual, though none the less real; but the saints thus reigning may be commissioned to appear on earth in some such way as angels appeared in former dispensations. The outbreak which follows the Millennium is couched in language borrowed from certain passages in the Old Testament (see especially Ezek. **38**) and will furnish their true and final fulfilment. But this outbreak is set forth as if it were the last permitted effort of Satan, and the ultimate destruction of the powers of evil is revealed at its close.

Concurrent epochs. If the view of the Millennium here given satisfies the requirements of the passage, we must still ask whether we are right in adjusting it to the period of the Restitution of Israel. It has often been noticed that the *Parousia* itself is not mentioned in the vision (Rev. **20**) or in those which immediately precede it. But on turning to the early chapters of the Revelation we find that, though the word itself is not used, *Parousia* passages abound (see **1.** 7; **2.** 25; **3.** 11, 21; **11.** 15). There are indeed some students, whose names and learning demand respect, who believe that we are in the Millennium now, that Satan is now bound, and that the vision of the reigning of the saints refers to the spread of Christian principles,* But our Lord seems to teach very definitely that the *Parousia* succeeds the "times of the Gentiles" and is not contemporary with them;

---

* On Augustine's view, see *infra*, p. 146.

and the "times of the Gentiles," which are certainly running on now, can hardly be described as Millennial.

On the whole the view most consistent with the New Testament, taken together, is that there are yet to be revealed, on and after the *Parousia*, two concurrent epochs which are ushered in by the Restitution of Israel upon earth and the First Resurrection. Those who have part in the First Resurrection share in Christ's spiritual dominion for a thousand years, *i.e.* for a very long period, and this is their training for the eternal Kingdom of God which will begin when Christ hands over the two-fold kingdom to the Father (1 Cor. 15. 28).

Students have often been struck with the contrast between the glowing descriptions of future earthly blessedness in the Old Testament, and the uphill path of antagonism against evil, and fortitude under persecution, which is the burden of the New Testament. But the bright prospect hinted at by Christ and His Apostles, and portrayed in Rev. 20, solves the apparent inconsistency. We must wait till the *Parousia*, and then the older predictions will be fulfilled—perhaps not literally and yet really and completely. When Christ comes again He will appear "unto salvation" (Heb. 9. 28). Then "all Israel will be saved" (Rom. 11. 26). Then the Lord will be, in a sense we cannot realise, not only a light to lighten the Gentiles, but the glory of His people Israel (Luke 2. 32). Then the tabernacle of David, which Amos and St. James spoke of, will be resuscitated (Amos 9. 11, 12 ; Acts 15. 16, 17), and David's throne will be established for ever, *i.e.* as long as the dispensation lasts (Luke 1. 33). Then Paradise will be regained ; and the narrow way will become broad, for Satanic power will be restricted.

This will be the time which the Lord calls "the Regeneration," when the Apostles shall judge Israel under their

Lord, and when the saints shall judge the world (Matt. **19.** 28; 1 Cor. **6.** 2; comp. Dan. **7.** 22).

As we meditate on the prospect many questions press for a solution :—

The Advent premillennial.

(*a.*) Is it quite certain that the Lord's return is pre-millennial according to the Scriptures? The Scotch school of prophetic students and some others have strongly opposed this view. They believe that the Millennium is arrived at by slow degrees through the gradual evangelisation of the world, and that it means the triumph of Christian principles, and that when things are at their very best Christ will return. This view, however, hardly seems to adjust itself to the requirements of the Scripture or to the revelation of the painful outbreak at the close of the Millennium. In fact, it is difficult to read the view into Rev. **20** at all. Augustine's view, which is expressed very frankly and with great moderation, deserves respectful mention. Repelled by the extreme material ideas of earlier millennarians, he reverts to the idea set forth in our Lord's own teaching. The first resurrection is the spiritual change which is experienced by the believer who is passed from death into life (John **5.** 24). The binding of Satan is the binding of "the strong man" (Matt. **12.** 29). The thousand years is the period between Christ's first coming and His second coming to judge the world. In Augustine's day (circ. 400 A.D.) there was an idea abroad that the Christian Church would only last 365 years; but he showed that the period in question, dating from the Day of Pentecost, was already past, and that men were seeing before their eyes the growth and triumph of Christianity. He considered the thousand years to be a round number, being the cube of ten, and not to be restricted exactly or literally. With regard to the subsequent outbreak, he held it would be the rise of antichrist, who should be a violent opponent of Christianity for three years and a half, and who should be destroyed by the Lord in His *Parousia*.

This view was held with some modifications by the late Bishop Wordsworth, of Lincoln, and it is to be distinguished from the view of Dr. David Brown and other Scotch interpreters, and from that of the leading Wesleyan writers, who look forward to the day when all the world shall be brought under Christian influence, and shall welcome the Lord on His return.*

(*b.*) Is there a physical catastrophe affecting the surface of the earth, somewhat analogous to the formation of a new geological stratum, at the ushering in of the Millennium? Some passages incline one to the affirmative, but there are considerations which make anything like a world-wide physical catastrophe improbable, if not impossible. There will doubtless be great changes, material as well as spiritual, at the time of the revelation of Christ in glory. But there will not be any such terrestrial convulsions as would block the continuity of the human race. These are reserved for a later stage. *Physical changes.*

(*c.*) Granting that the Millennium is to come, and that Israel is to be a restored people, and that certain saints will at the same time attain to the First Resurrection, will earthly affairs be carried on as now? Will there be masters and servants, coal-miners and scavengers, railways and trams? Will the elect saints rule over (*i.e.* exert a spiritual influence over) the non-elect people who happen to be still living in different parts of the world, certain cities (or, shall we say *parishes?*) being allotted to each? Will the Jewish sacrificial system be restored? Will the risen Patriarchs be visibly introduced into their promised inheritance? And how will it be with all these people at the final Judgment? These are *Millennial life.*

---

* See, *e.g.* the late William Arthur's *Tongue of Fire.*

not a hundredth part of the questions which occur to us as we contemplate the prospect. But our absolute ignorance need not shake our convictions. Whatever God ordains will speedily seem natural.*

The final outbreak.

(*d*.) Taking the Millennium to be "the Day of the Lord," and assenting to the view that He comes at the beginning of the day, then we understand that He hands over the kingdom at the end of the day (1 Cor. **15**); but how will this adjust itself to the outbreak which follows the Millennium? One is inclined to answer with the hymn, "God is His own interpreter, and He will make it plain." However we explain away the Millennium still this difficulty faces us. It is not the last chapter of human history, though it is the last but one, and it confirms us in the conviction that this earth, which has been the scene of so much sin and suffering, is to witness greater things than we can conceive, and that Christ shall be acknowledged as the true King of Nations.

Early Christian views.

The earliest Christians seem to have held a very simple view of the Millennium. Justin Martyr, in his dialogue with Trypho, says (§ 81): "There was a certain man with us whose name was John, one of the Apostles of Christ, who prophesied, by a revelation that was made to him, that those who believed in our Christ would dwell in Jerusalem for a thousand years, and that afterwards the general and eternal resurrection and judgment of all men should take place." Papias says that "There will be a thousand years after the resurrection from the dead,† when the reign of Christ will be established bodily on this earth." Irenæus held the view, which seems to have been originally Jewish, that after 6,000 years of human history a change shall be brought about (*Against Heresies*, v. 28);

---

* See W. D. Heath's *Future Kingdom of Christ*.

† See Eusebius, *Ch. Hist.* iii. 39. It is noteworthy that Eusebius here attributes to Papias the expression "*from the dead*" as distinguished from the ordinary doctrine of the resurrection *of* the dead.

then shall come what he calls "the hallowed seventh day," "the times of the kingdom," when the promised inheritance shall be restored to Abraham (chap. xxx.). This, he says, is the resurrection of the just, and of the kingdom which is the commencement of incorruption, by means of which kingdom those who are worthy are gradually to comprehend (or partake of) the Divine nature, receiving the promise of the inheritance which God promised to the fathers and to reign in it. Thus, in the very creation in which they toiled or were afflicted they will receive the reward of their suffering. He cites Papias, whom he calls "a hearer of John and a companion of Polycarp," in favour of this view, as also certain "elders who saw John the disciple of the Lord" (chap. xxxiii.), and quotes the words of John, who says the very same in the Revelation: "Blessed and holy is he who has part in the First Resurrection" (chap. xxxiv.; comp. also the close of chap. xxxvi.).

CHAPTER XIX.

CHRIST AND ANTICHRIST.

Opposition to God.

THE gift of choice or will which has been bestowed on man and on some other beings not only throws great responsibility on them, but also makes it possible that they should set themselves against the will of Him by whose permission they live. The results of such rebellion must have been foreseen and provided against from the beginning. Meanwhile, the historical fact has to be faced that all through the human period, so far as it is covered by the Old Testament, we read of opposition to God's will. There were human adversaries—rebellious subjects—on earth, and there was the Adversary, or Satan (השטן), in the spirit-world. This opposition was partly directed against the law of righteousness, partly against the true Israelites, in whom that law of righteousness was in a measure embodied, and partly against the supremacy of the God of Israel Himself. We know very little about the forces of evil, and nothing about the origin of evil in the spirit-world as distinguished from the results of temptation recorded in history and realised in experience. Physical science does not help us here. We have nothing to go by but Scripture, and the contemplation of the workings of evil in our own nature.

There are a few passages in the Old Testament which point to the rising up of some special opponents in certain periods of history, who should seek to draw to themselves the allegiance due to God, and should fight against His people simply because they were His people (see Isai. **14**; Ezek. **38, 39**; Dan. **7, 8, 11**). But these may be passed over here, and we will proceed to the New Testament.

CHRIST AND ANTICHRIST.

Our Lord, early in His teaching, bade His followers to beware of false prophets; He also prepared them for persecution, hatred, and death for His Name's sake. In the Acts we get plenty of illustrations of the spirit of persecution, and some indications are given of the rise of false teachers (see Acts 20. 29, 30). On turning to the Epistles we are struck with the fact that many of them bear the marks of having been written in the times of persecution and strong opposition to the truth. Satan himself is regarded as the chief opponent. This early antagonism to Christianity was partly Jewish, partly heathen, partly philosophic, partly sensual. Germs of strange heresies were in the air. Already, says St. John, there were many antichrists, *i.e.* many who denied the truth of God and of Christ. But beyond these false teachers there was to be one in particular (1 John 2. 18; 4. 3) who would lead the people astray in matters of life and doctrine. St. John's prophetic utterance might point to secularism, to infidelity, or to some form of Gnosticism,* and to its attendant iniquities. St. Peter and St. Jude also tell of heretical false teachers who would combine covetousness with erroneous doctrine (2 Pet. 2. 1–3; comp. St. Jude's Epistle, *passim*). Both these writers describe the opponents as scoffers or mockers who should walk after their ungodly lusts in the latter days.

Opposition to Christ.

St. Paul is more full and explicit on the subject. Besides his frequent references to the need of watchfulness against error, secularism, and sensuality, there were special instructions contained in his Second Epistle to the Thessalonians. In the 2nd chapter we are told that there was to be the Apostasy or falling away from Christ; then in connexion with it there would come to the front a leader of evil, who is called the

The Man of Sin.

---

* On this subject see Mansel's *Lectures on the Gnostic Heresies.*

man of sin, *i.e.* the sinful man, one who embodied sin in himself to an exceptional degree; he is also called the son of perdition—destructive and to be destroyed—the adversary of God, lifting himself up in opposition to all true worship, practically superseding God and acting as if he himself were a god (2 Thess. **2.** 3, 4). Further, he is called the lawless one, who would be manifested and come to the front when certain hindrances or difficulties were removed, and who would be brought to nought by the Lord at His *Parousia*. The work of this strange being is described as Satanic, as accompanied with false signs, miracles, and mighty works, his *Parousia* being thus a sort of counterpart or caricature of Christ's, and his powers being exercised for the propagation of unrighteousness and lies. Many will be caught by his deceit and will believe his lies, partly through ignorance and partly because his system will pander to their fleshly lusts (*vv.* 8–11).

It is noteworthy that these things which Paul wrote he had already spoken about orally during his first brief visit to Thessalonica (*v.* 5). Probably he unfolded the same prospect in other places also. There can be very little doubt, in fact, that this subject formed part of his regular teaching, and that St. John's words, "Ye have heard that the antichrist shall come," is a brief embodiment of a special line of teaching which was set forth by all the Apostles.

Paul and Daniel.

To what, then, does St. Paul refer? His language is evidently taken in part from Dan. **11.** 37. This notable chapter of Daniel gives a sketch of the future, from the time of the Persian Empire till the time of the end. Large periods of time are omitted when unnecessary for the purpose, *e.g.* 150 years are passed over between the 2nd and 3rd verse, according to the ordinary interpretation of the chapter. The days of Antiochus Epiphanes, who comes to the front

CHRIST AND ANTICHRIST.

in the 21st verse, are blended with the period of the downfall of Jerusalem and the Temple in *v.* 31; and "the time of the end" is foreseen in *v.* 35. Then we are introduced to the king who exalts himself against God and honours the god of fortresses (R.V.). He thus appears to be both despotic and antitheistic. The Apostles believed that this personage was yet to come, and that as all true theism is gathered up in Christ, so all antitheism is embodied in antichrist—this name signifying either a substitute for Christ or an opponent to Him.

How do we stand towards this prophecy now? Before answering, the first thing to be decided is whether it is a system which is predicted, or whether it is a person. The language of St. Paul is strongly in favour of its being a person; and we know by experience that all "new departures," whether for good or evil, owe their success to personal influence. Accordingly we look through the centuries in order to find out any traces of fulfilment, whether elementary or complete.

The early Churches were distracted by heresies which *Mohammed and the Pope.* ranked themselves more or less under the name Gnostic; but no one notable person came to the front in those days who at all answered to Daniel's description of the wilful king, or to St. Paul's description of the man of sin. In the 7th century Mohammedanism rose in the East and Romanism in the West. Each involves serious departure from the truth of Christ. Each is to some extent antichristian. Mohammed claimed to be the promised Comforter and the Prophet who was to represent Christ; and the Bishop of Rome claimed also to be the vicar of Christ upon earth. One view was propagated by the sword for a thousand years and still possesses millions of bigoted adherents; the other, as it grew in power and pride, sought to stifle opposition against itself by every possible means, including war and diplomacy, torture and the stake.

These rival systems have been a blight on vital Christianity, and have stood in the way of the evangelisation of the world for many centuries. It is no wonder that commentators have referred to one or the other of them as fulfilling the predictions of St. Paul; and they do undoubtedly point in that direction. But it is observable that hitherto neither of these systems have answered all the requirements of the passage. Both have had checks, and have had to advance in new directions, while both minister to false teaching, and are practically antichristian, yet they are at the opposite poles of error. Hereafter, according to St. Paul, there will be a culmination of falsehood under one head, who will emerge at the time of the end, and after doing his subtle, mischievous, and cruel work, will be destroyed by the Lord at His *Parousia*. Such seems the natural interpretation of the Scripture; but the solution of this, together with many other problems, has to be left open at present.

The Apocalypse. We naturally turn to the Book of the Revelation at this point to see if it throws any light on the question. Can we find in it the vision of some power which should counterfeit Christianity, should be really both despotic and atheistic whilst keeping under cover of religion, and which should come to a head towards the time of the end? First, we see mischief brewing, in the letters to the seven Churches. Then we see all earthly things drawing to a close during the breaking of the seven Seals and the sounding of the seven Trumpets. This takes us to the end of the 11th chapter. Then two remarkable appearances are recorded. There is the woman clothed with the sun, with the moon under her feet, and a crown of twelve stars on her head (comp. Gen. **37**. 9);

and over against her is the dragon with seven heads and ten crowned horns. The first of these we naturally take to be Israel, and the child she brings forth is Christ.* The second is explained in the context as Satan. Failing in destroying Christ he persecutes both Israel and the Lord's followers. So far all is fulfilled.

In the 13th chapter the characteristics of the Dragon are found embodied in the Beast, who is generally supposed to represent some great world-power, *e.g.* Rome. His seventh head is wounded to death, but recovers. This seventh head thus strangely restored assumes despotic power over the nations and blasphemes God. Then a lamb-like, two-horned beast is seen, in alliance with the Beast, deceiving people by false miracles. The numerical value of the letters which compose his name is 666, which is "the number of a man." This lamb-like counterfeit of the true Lamb is subsequently called the "false prophet." Yet another vision is recorded, in the 17th chapter; it is a woman; she is called a whore, because she has broken her covenant with God. She is rich, vile, and drunk with the blood of martyrs of Jesus.

Putting these visions together, we have Satan the great mischief maker; the imperialism of Rome carrying out the Satanic policy of persecution; the false prophet doing the same in a more subtle way; the woman, *i.e.* the unfaithful Church (?), utilising imperial power to destroy the true followers of Christ. It can hardly be doubted that we have here developed in vision what St. Paul taught in veiled and sober prose. The subsequent history of the Church of Rome gives us a painful commentary on the text, though it is still doubtful whether an individual leader is not portrayed as destined

---

* Of course there are other interpretations of this and of every other vision.

to appear as the embodiment of many-sided evil. That "woman," on whom so much attention is concentrated, is mystically called "Babylon" (Rev. **17**. 18), partly because of the strong secular element in her nature, imperialism and false religion being combined in her, and partly because her downfall is as great and terrible as that of the ancient empire of the East. Her end is destruction, for the ten horns (*i.e.* the subdivision of the empire) bring her to desolation (chap. **17**. 15, etc.).

At length the child, whose birth had been narrated in chap. **12**. 5, and who was destined to rule the nations with the rod of iron, comes forth from heaven to judge and make war; and secular imperialism, which had already, according to the vision, cast off the sway of false religion, perishes (chap. **19**. 15–21).

This tremendous catastrophe is associated with the *Parousia* of Christ by St. Paul in 2 Thess. **2**, and it therefore naturally prepares the way for the Millennium in Rev. **20**, when the Dragon himself, the ultimate cause of all earth's trouble, is dealt with, first being bound, and then (1,000 years afterwards) being cast into the lake of fire, the final embers of antagonism to Christ being thus stamped out.

Putting these and other passages together, and deducting as much as seems reasonable from the visionary language of the Apocalypse, we cannot but see a pictorial prophecy of the great conflict between truth and error, the one embodied in Christ, the other in an amalgamated system of secularism, false teaching, sensuality, and persecution, probably developed in their extreme form under one head. The final triumph of truth and righteousness over all evil is also clearly revealed.

View of Antichrist the early Church. The revelation of antichrist was a matter of intense interest to the early Church. Most of the teachers in the 3rd and 4th centuries seem to have put together the passages from Daniel, St. Paul, and the Revelation, to which reference has just been made. They usually considered that his ascendency was to be permitted for the mystical three and a half years, the half week of Daniel. Some, *e.g.* Irenæus, associated him with the period before the Millennium; others identified his rise with the outbreak which is to occur after the Millennium.

There is a work by the celebrated Hippolytus, Bishop of Portus, on *Christ and Antichrist*, in which he urges the necessity of carefully studying what is said on the subject in the Holy Scriptures. The Roman Empire, he says, constitutes the Fourth Beast of Daniel; the toes of the feet are "emblems" of the kingdoms that are yet to rise; and the "little horn" is antichrist, whom he expected (in common with many others) to spring out of the Tribe of Dan. He proceeds to quote John "the apostle and disciple of the Lord," citing long passages from the 17th and 18th of the Revelation, together with some of the earlier chapters, and takes Antiochus Epiphanes as a sort of type of the antichristian, two-horned lamb who heals the wounded head of the Beast. Following Irenæus he is inclined to identify the number 666 with the word *Lateinos*, as the Latins were then holding the imperial power (§ 50), and he introduced St. Paul's utterance as to be fulfilled in the rise and fall of this Satanic and antichristian personage.

The infidel Celsus seems to have mocked at the thought of antichrist; but Origen answers him without hesitation, and shows from Scripture that there is to be a personal head of evil in the same sense as Christ is the impersonation of righteousness, and that he will deceive the human race but subsequently perish.

Lactantius (*Inst.* vii. 17, etc.) describes antichrist as an nfidel king who shall falsely call himself Christ, and shall fight against the truth, but shall pay the penalty of his crimes; after which shall come the Millennium, the 6,000 years of human history having been completed, and the city of Rome having fallen. Tertullian also puts antichristian oppression before the Millennium in his treatise against Marcion (iii. 24; v. 12).

Augustine's views of the Millennium naturally lead him to put the period of antichrist at the close of all, and he therefore identifies it with the final outbreak before the last judgment. He calls it "the last persecution," but he refuses to be tied to the theory then already prevailing that there would be only a fixed number of persecutions answering to the ten persecuting Emperors—Nero, Domitian, Trajan, Antoninus, Severus, Maximin, Decius, Valerian, Aurelian, and Diocletian with Maximian (*City of God*, xviii. 52). He refers with approval to Jerome's commentary on Daniel in connexion with the fourth (or Roman) Beast; and he thinks that the ten kings stand for the total number of kings who precede antichrist.

We possess a commentary on the Revelation by Victorinus, Bishop of Petau, dating from about A.D. 300. It is simple and to the point. In dealing with Rev. 7 and 11 he introduces Elias as yet to come before antichrist, and for three and a half years he, and perhaps Moses, will witness, and then be slain by antichrist, whose kingdom will last over a similar period. The Beast stands for Rome, from whom antichrist springs. His view of the Millennium is the same as was adopted a hundred years later by Augustine, and he holds that the antichristian spirit will be revealed in a personal opponent to the Church during the three and a half years which precede the final Judgment.

CHAPTER XX.

THE FINAL JUDGMENT AND THAT WHICH IS BEYOND.

WE have attempted to show from Scripture that the *Parousia* of Christ is connected (*a*) with the ushering in of the Israelite kingdom in its final stage, (*b*) with the reign of the saints, (*c*) with the downfall of error and opposition. These great movements seem to be connected both morally and chronologically. They are seen together, as the sufferings and reign of Christ were seen together in the Old Testament, but considerable periods of time may be covered in the course of carrying out the Divine programme.

It only remains for us cautiously to lift the veil a little further, and to express in outline or in rudimentary language what Prophecy has to say concerning the destiny of the individual and the world at large after the human period as we now know it has run out.

1. Scripture teaches us that death, which meets us at every turn in our present existence, was not originally intended to close man's career. Other creatures below us in type live their little life and pass away. They have served their purpose; but the Divine intention concerning man was far different. It is no idle boast that the world was made for man; a large portion of its products, *e.g.* coal, would otherwise be useless; but the real question to be answered is, What was man made for? He is placed at the border-land of two worlds, the physical and the spiritual. His footsteps are planted at birth a long way up the ladder or scale of existence, and he might

State of the dead.

ascend still higher. But the Adversary beguiled our first parents, and when they fell we all fell, by the law of heredity. We Christians believe, on reasons that will bear the fullest investigation, that Christ, the Son of God, was manifested that He might undo the mischief thus done to the Race; and it is the main province of the Bible to affirm and illustrate the Divine method of regenerating the children of men through the truth of Christ. But death still invades us Christians, even though it has lost its sting. Those, however, who truly believe in Christ, whilst bidding farewell to all else when they depart, do not bid farewell to Christ. Asleep so far as the world is concerned, they are awake to Him. Being disembodied they may fairly be supposed to be inactive, and the conditions of time and space which are essential to us may barely exist to them. At length the congregation of the dead will be aroused, the number made up, and those who are asleep in Christ will be awakened. A new and thrilling consciousness will stir within them, and in the twinkling of an eye they will find themselves in organised, though spiritual, bodies thronging the spiritual palace of their Lord and in attendance on His movements. The judgment or adjustment of positions which follows will be overwhelming in solemnity; but those to whom the unveiled sight of the King is most precious here will then be most happy, and will find themselves able to feel, to think, to act, and to express themselves, to an extent and in ways which are utterly inconceivable to us at present.

The Judgment.

2. The reign of glory called the Millennium appears to follow; but what is beyond that? There is a more universal judgment which the Bible as a whole prepares us for, and which the moral sense or conscience of man approves and demands. The messages of Scripture concerning this judgment are brief but impressive. Only a few points may be

touched upon here. Let us shortly enumerate the most noteworthy :—

i. First, although God is the Judge of all the earth by universal acknowledgment, yet the final destiny of the individual members of the human race depends upon the decision of the Lord Jesus, to whom all judicial authority is delegated by the Father.

ii. While nations as such have their judgment in this world, individuals are to be dealt with in a day or period yet to come, at the last stage of the last day, when the present phase of earthly existence comes to an end.

iii. The principles on which men's destinies will be decided are laid down clearly in Scripture. Foremost among these there is the principle of *Retribution*, embodied in the formula "according to their works"; and by "works" we are to understand the products of man's free-will. These are what form our character. As Christians we are justified by faith; but we are judged according to works, which are the fruit and test of our real faith. Some similar test will be applied to all the world.

iv. There is also the principle of *Equity*. God takes everything into account; our heredity, our environment, our knowledge, our opportunities, and the way in which we have used, neglected, or resisted His grace. No two cases are really alike. He knows not only what we have done, but what we should have done under other circumstances. Comp. Matt. **10**. 15; **11**. 22, 24; **12**. 41, 42. He who does not break the bruised reed nor quench the smoking flax may safely be trusted to do what is right.

v. There is another principle, founded on the fact that the Lamb of God bore the sins of the world. Whatever is forgivable will be forgiven. Whatever can be cleansed will be cleansed. Whatever is indelible will remain. What use have we made of the grace of God so far as it has been revealed to us? This seems to be the question of questions; and it will be applicable in some sense to the world at large.

vi. There will be the utmost *variety* in the lot of those who are judged. We gather that in the case of Christians, those who run with patience the race set before them will receive from the Righteous Judge a crown. It will be a crown of life (Jas. 1. 12), a crown of righteousness (2 Tim. 4. 8), and a crown of glory (1 Pet. 5. 4). These crowns or rewards will not be like the old garlands which so speedily faded away, but will be permanent marks of Christ's approbation of His faithful soldiers and servants. And as one star differeth from another in glory so it will be with regard to the reward. Men will reap according as they have sown. Thus, we are taught that the reward for purity is spiritual vision; the reward for faithfulness in little things will be an opportunity of exercising stewardship on a larger scale; the reward for unselfishness will be an increased power and scope for exercising the spirit of love.

As there will be varieties in position so there will be in degree. Paul sought to present every man perfect in Christ (Col. 1. 28), but he probably failed to do so. There are many degrees of spiritual temperature in Christian souls. So far as this is owing to congenital physical lethargy it will drop off at death, but so far as it is owing to culpable negligence we shall recognise the fact and the result at the Great Day, and so with all other phases of life and character.

It may seem to us and to our limited understanding impossible to deal separately and variously with the million million of people, old and young, who have lived upon earth; but there will be no difficulty with God.

vii. So far as can be ascertained from Scripture, the life that we live upon earth, and not anything which befalls us in the intermediate state, forms the basis and supplies the materials for judgment. The things done through the agency of the body (2 Cor. 5. 10) are what will be taken into consideration. Probation is over after death; seed-sowing is ended; the account of our stewardship is made up. The disembodied condition of man does not seem to offer any sphere for the development of character. Certainly Scripture gives us no hint of Purgatory, but rather goes the other way. And so far as we can see, the principle which applies to those who rise in the First Resurrection will apply to the second also. All will reap what they have sown in this life. The searchlight of the Judge will be turned on every soul, and each will instinctively, perhaps automatically, give in his account, and it will then be seen whether he is among the saved or the lost, among those who are within or those that are without.

viii. The physical condition of those who stand before the great White Throne as distinguished from those who share the First Resurrection is not described in Scripture. The true Christian who lives for his Master here will share his Master's condition hereafter; but of the rest there is no clear announcement. St. Paul says (2 Tim. 2. 20) that "in a great house there are not only vessels of gold and silver, but also of wood and of earth, and some to honour and some to dishonour." So doubtless there will be gradations of physical and mental structure, and perhaps of permanence also, in the case of the non-Christian members of the human race. What is described as "eternal destruction" (2 Thess. 1. 9) is for the enemies of Christ, and what is called "eternal punishment" (Matt. 25. 46) is for those who have not a grain of love in their composition. The first half of the 2nd chapter of the Romans is the most full and important Apostolic message on this subject, and it applies primarily to the self-righteous Jew.

After all, dismissal from Christ's presence is the most serious of penalties which can befall the children of men. Various expressions are used which indicate the sad position of those who are thus dismissed. They endure the fire of Divine wrath, which none can quench, and which must inevitably do the work which God intends. They are in Gehenna or Hell. This position or condition expresses a Jewish thought that takes its name from the valley of Hinnom, which was the scene both of the people's sin and of their punishment (Jer. 7. 31–33), so that it embodies the idea of retribution. They are outside the heavenly city and the Divine light of Christ and the possibilities of healthy activity, and endure the bitterness of remorse. In a word, their condition so far as it is revealed at present is both hopeless, permanent, inevitable. Beyond that we can see nothing.

There are no indications in Scripture as to their number or as to their proportion to the saved; but the unpardonable rejectors of grace may prove to be very few indeed. In any case the severity of God's dealing with them is owing to the fact that they have taken their fate into their own hands, and have judged themselves unworthy of everlasting life. It may be that they will be an object-lesson to other races and to other worlds.*

The new earth.

4. There is one more glimpse of the final condition of things, and it is mainly physical. It has to do with the dwelling-place of redeemed man and his ultimate surroundings.

Our experience of the present state of things leads us to the conviction that hereafter, as here, there must be a divinely-arranged adaptation of the saints' abode to their own structure, and *vice versa*. Man's body now is of the dust

---

* The contents of this section are mainly taken from a work written many years ago and now rarely obtainable, viz. *Dies Iræ*, a discussion of the principles of Divine Judgment.

THE FINAL JUDGMENT AND THAT WHICH IS BEYOND.

of the earth; the materials of which it is composed are the same as those of which all nature is composed, though in varying proportions. But if man was prepared for earth, earth itself had already been prepared for man. When our Lord was about to leave the world, He said, "In My Father's house are many mansions . . . . I go to prepare a place for you . . . . I will come again and receive you to Myself, that where I am there ye may be also" (John 14. 2, 3). The preparation of the world for man took many ages: How long does the preparation of this new place in God's mansions take? As we are taught that all things came into being originally through the agency of the *Logos*, so we learn from our Lord's lips it will be hereafter; and if there was a relationship between the materials of which earth is composed, and those of which man's body is composed, so it must surely be hereafter.

Pursuing this thought, we look to the Scriptures to see what they tell us concerning the resurrection body of the saint. In 1 Cor. **15**. 35, etc., we have some important instruction on the matter. Two questions are supposed to be asked: first, How or by what process are the dead to be raised? secondly, With what sort of body are they to come? The first question is answered by the analogy of germination, which involves previous death or disintegration—an analogy already referred to by our Lord (John **12.** 24). The second question is answered categorically:— *The spiritual body.*

i. God decides what sort of body each kind of seed shall produce.

ii. There are distinctions between the texture of the flesh of different kinds of creatures.

iii. As there are bodies adapted for dwellers on earth, so there are bodies adapted for dwellers in heaven; and the glory or brightness of each is different.

iv. Similarly, there are distinctions in brilliancy between sun and moon and stars, these last being of varied magnitude (*i.e.* brilliancy).

v. In the same way there is a vast distinction, amounting to a contrast, between the body which the saint lays down at death and the body he assumes at resurrection. The one is liable to decay, dishonour, weakness; the other is undecaying, glorious, endued with power. The one is *psychical*, being animated by a living soul, in conformity with the original structure of the first Adam; the other is *pneumatical*, being inspired by a life-giving spirit, after the type of the last Adam. The first man, the type of the present bodily life, is of the dust of the earth; the second man, the type of the future bodily life, is the Lord from heaven.

This is indeed a most instructive and stirring revelation. It points to a body which is not liable to decay. Such a body would be relieved of a great deal of burden and distress; it would need no blood, which is the great carrier of reinforcements through the system, and which conveys to the lungs for combustion all decaying and used-up material. A body, largely relieved of the digestive system, together with lungs, and heart, and arteries, and veins, is thus suggested. What is there left as the Temple of the Spirit? The head, which is the recipient and giver forth of impressions and actions, and the limbs, which are the servants of the head. These are to be powerful and *pneumatical*. The senses—or whatever answers to them—will be endued with vastly increased capacity, as will the mind, which is at the back of them. Perhaps the barriers between the senses will be broken down, when all that belongs to the soul will be dominated by the spirit.* The same may be true of the other departments of the resurrection body.

---

* On the distinction between soul and spirit see *Old Testament Synonyms*, chap. iv.

In dealing with the same subject, our Lord reveals two important additional truths. One is that there will be no sexual distinctions in heaven; the other is that in this and other respects, the risen saints are as the angels or equal to the angels. The body of the saint will thus be like the body of the angel. It will be celestial, but capable of manifestation upon earth. Illustrations of angelic appearances run through the whole Bible, and are consistent throughout. They could appear as men, they could even eat and drink as men, but earth was not their home—this was in heaven or the spirit-world.

Our Lord's resurrection condition is manifestly the type to which the bodies of the risen saints are to be conformed (Phil. 3. 21), and as His was glorious, so will theirs be. It was necessary, for evidential purposes, that He should be identified by His disciples after His resurrection, and therefore His body assumed for the time a condition as near the earthly body as could be. And yet it was not an earthly body. It had been changed. Students of the Gospel narrative do not seem always to have noticed two remarkable facts. First, although many saw the Lord after His resurrection, yet no one saw Him rise. Why not? Because resurrection really means the change of a body from the psychical to the pneumatical condition. In the Lord's case all the materials which formed the psychical body went through the marvellous transformation which caused it to become a spiritual body like that of the angels. He became, so far, a human angel, though He was more. Secondly, the spiritualisation of the psychical body of Christ is attested by the fact that the wrappings in which He had been enveloped before being laid in the grave had not been disturbed at His resurrection. It is needless to point out that they could not well be unrolled within the narrow compass of the sepulchre,

Our Lord's body.

especially when we remember the amount of myrrh and aloes which was included (John 19. 39). The body would, under ordinary circumstances, be taken out to be unrolled. But this had not happened. The wrappings still lay within the tomb, and the coil for His head was still coiled up. It was the sight of this that made Peter and John believe that the Lord was risen.

Etherealisation.

Spiritualisation seems akin to etherealisation. This thought has been developed in two remarkable books. One was by the celebrated lay theologian and essayist, Isaac Taylor, the elder. It is entitled *The Physical Theory of Another Life*, and though highly speculative, is exceedingly suggestive. It was published so far back as 1836. The other is entitled *The Unseen Universe*, and follows on very much the same lines, though written without reference to the older book. It is the work of two of the most eminent men of the modern school, Professors Tait and Balfour Stewart. These authorities do not contend that ether is spirit or spirit ether, but that the ethereal condition is the type and perhaps the embodiment of the spiritual, which in its turn is akin to the very essence of the Divine Being.

Adaptation of earth to man.

5. The question now before us is, How far this world in which we live, or any other world, can be prepared as the dwelling-place of incorruptible ethereal beings? Certainly, as it is now, the earth hardly seems adapted to be the home of the angels. But we are familiarised all through Scripture with the fact that the present state of things is transient. It exists for a purpose. It is the training-ground of the children of Adam. It supplies the material scaffolding for a spiritual edifice.

The world that is to be must be in harmony with the resurrection body of the saints. Consequently, it must not be subject to decay. Now this is exactly the prospect held out in Scripture with respect to the new state of things. We read in Rom. **8.** 21 that creation is to be delivered from the bondage of decay, and to be brought into the liberty of the glory of the children of God. And St. Peter describes the inheritance of the saints as incorruptible, unpolluted, and unfading (1 Pet. **1.** 4). He adds that it is kept in heaven for us, as we are kept on earth for it. The stirring description given in Rev. **21** and **22** adjusts itself to these more simple and elementary passages.

It must be frankly admitted that the mind of man cannot conceive the future state of things. In a measure, it is possible to picture up the risen condition of the saints because of the indications given above. We may also get an idea of the endless variety and interests of eternity when we meditate on the revelation given us in the starry heavens; for perhaps the millions of millions of stars may each be in its time a home for created sentient beings, each coming into existence when needed, and passing out when its work is done.

We can also conceive that this earth and the rest of the solar family may be done away with. Science, indeed, tells us that it must be so. But when we try to disentangle ourselves from figurative and poetic language, and to emerge beyond the twilight of negatives into the full light of positive description, we fail. But we have all we want, for we have Christ,—and He has said, " Heaven and earth shall pass away, but My word shall not pass away."

CHAPTER XXI.

CONCLUDING OBSERVATIONS.

IN closing the present discussion it may be permitted to review the steps which have been taken, and the results which have been attained.

Survey of the book.

i. All the way through, the Bible has been taken as a book of authority, written in many ages and contributed to by many minds, but all under the inspiring direction of one Master, Who has adopted Prophecy as His method of revealing His will and purposes. It has not been thought necessary to go into details touching the composition, age, and authorship of the Books. They are taken as giving us an ancient and trustworthy record. On any view of them which reasonable men will accept, the least that can be said is that while the Old Testament testifies to Christ, He in His turn testifies to it, and History testifies to both.

ii. Certain fundamental ideas concerning God are taken for granted, *e.g.* that He is the living, personal, eternal Author of the universe, and the Father of the human race, and that the inspiration of the Prophets to see, to speak, and to write, came from Him, and is in accordance with His essential nature.

iii. The leading facts and phenomena presented by Biblical prediction have been surveyed and enumerated.

iv. Prophetic terminology has been systematically discussed, its grammar traced out as far as practicable, and its chief characteristic expressions and ideas examined.

v. The scientific method of interpreting the language of Biblical prediction, whether fulfilled or unfulfilled, has been set forth.

CONCLUDING OBSERVATIONS. 171

vi. The most notable subjects of prophecy, *e.g.* those which have to do with Israel and with the Messiah, have been selected for more detailed examination, though in bare outline only.

vii. The yet unfulfilled elements in Scriptural prophecy have been reserved till the last, and while certain conclusions have been counted as sure, other matters have been left open.

While dealing with these important subjects, the conviction, entertained for many years, has been deepening in the writer's mind, that prediction is an essential element in Revelation, and that we lose a great blessing if we disregard it. As St. Peter says, "We do well to take heed to it" (2 Pet. 1. 19), for it is like " a light shining in a dark place." And so says St. John (Rev. 1. 3), "Blessed is he that readeth and they that hear the words of this prophecy, and keep those things which are written therein." *Grandeur and difficulty of the study.*

There are, it is true, many perplexities, arising from various circumstances, which beset the student, but there is much to encourage us in our study. The nature of the things which the prophets set forth may be obscure, and even the order uncertain, but there is a grandeur and an impressiveness in what is revealed which we should be slow to neglect. We may not have a fixed programme of the future to announce to our friends,—certainly the present writer has no such programme; he has been discussing method rather than proclaiming events— but we get our reward. The providential rule of God, His moral government, His eternal supremacy over beings whom He has permitted to exist, despite their passive resistance and active antagonism to His will, His varied dealings with nations and individuals, lifting them up and casting them down, His preparation of earth for the abode of the blessed and for a more glorious manifestation of Himself in Christ than we can conceive—these are the principles stamped upon our minds with increasing clearness as we pursue our studies. Sometimes we are confounded by the slowness of the Divine processes as realised in History; at other times we are struck by their sureness. Our thoughts are often paralysed by their own limitations; they seem so different to God's thoughts; and at best we seem to see only the reflections of things and the enigmatical side of them (1 Cor. **13.** 12). But we need not despair. God's Word is written on a very large scale, and though it is so compactly in our hands it covers a great deal of historical and prophetical ground. There is no book like it in this respect. The fulfilment of prophecies in the past, whether national or individual, whether external or spiritual, justifies us in expecting a similar fulfilment in the future. History is the best commentary on prophecy. Elliott used Gibbon's *Decline and Fall of the Roman Empire* all the way through his work on the Apocalypse, and whilst we are by no means bound to follow him in all his conclusions, we cannot fail to respect and admire this part of his method. We proceed from the known to the unknown, from the way in which old prophecies have been fulfilled to the way in which the others which yet stand over are likely to receive their fulfilment. If the one class of prophecy was fulfilled literally, we expect that the other will be also. Even where we cannot trace the fulfilment of the past it will usually be found that this is owing to some imperfection or lack in existing historical record, or because certain conditions affecting the prophecy were altered.

The second coming of Christ.

The personal expectation of the second coming of the Lord Jesus Christ, which St. Paul and the other Apostles felt and taught, is a wonderful tonic for our spiritual life. It discourages laxity in life and teaching; it stirs us up to exercise self-discipline and diligence; it calls us to be pure, peaceable, and unworldly; it upholds us when we are cast down by the

CONCLUDING OBSERVATIONS. 173

prevalence of secularism and unbelief, or when we are suffering at the hand of the persecutor.

Is it really true that the Saviour is coming again? Is it true that we Christians must all be presented before Him? Is it true that He must decide on the destinies of each one of us, and that we must individually render to Him an account of our stewardship? And must the Jew, the Mohammedan, and the heathen do the same? Are there certain fixed principles according to which our future position is to be allotted? Will any one escape notice or evade judgment or be overlooked? Will the omniscience, the tender pity, the righteousness, the redeeming love of the heart-searcher be brought to bear on each case? Will the Son of Man, to whom all judgment is delegated, be equal to the tremendous task thus laid upon His shoulders? and will God be justified on that great day?

To these serious questions Scripture gives an unhesitating reply, and the answer has stamped itself on the creeds of Christendom. These are the things to make sure of, and it is vain to discuss other things till we have got these central truths concerning the future stamped upon our hearts and made operative in our lives.

When we get beyond them we find ourselves in a mist. *Perplexities as to details.* This is partly due to the difficulty created by the nature of figurative language; partly to chronological uncertainties; partly to the Millennial question, which cannot lightly be put aside, and which apparently parts the Resurrection and Judgment of a certain class from that of the rest by a period of a thousand years. We naturally shrink, except on clearest evidence, from interjecting this long period between two events which are frequently thrown together in one verse. We have, however, to remember that the case of the two advents of our Lord is somewhat similar. They seemed one in Old Testament days, but they have proved to be separated by some two thousand years. To go further back, the promises made to Abraham might naturally be expected to be fulfilled in a short time, but again a period of some two thousand years intervened before Peter could stand up and claim the fulfilment of God's promise in Christ. The question of the Millennium thus becomes a matter of authority and of interpretation. Its acceptance will probably be found to solve far more difficulties than it creates.

Butler on the world's future.

The most sober and profound of thinkers, Bishop Butler, in his chapter on the Moral Government of God (*Analogy*, i. 3), adumbrates the millennial condition and the restoration of the Jews as a leading nation, in words not easily to be improved upon. After pointing out the difficulties in the way of a virtuous and united social constitution now, he shows that there must be room for such a state of things within the compass of the material world (*i.e.* universe), and proceeds thus:—

"But let us return to the earth, our habitation, and suppose a kingdom or society of men upon it perfectly virtuous for a succession of many ages, to which, if you please, may be given a situation advantageous for universal monarchy. In such a state there would be no such thing as faction, but men of the greatest capacity would of course all along have the chief direction of affairs willingly yielded to them, and they would share it among themselves without envy. Each of these would have the part assigned to him to which his genius was peculiarly adapted; and others who had not any distinguished genius would be safe, and think themselves very happy by being under the protection and guidance of those who had . . . . Some would in a higher way contribute, but all would in some way contribute to the public prosperity; and in it each would enjoy the fruits of his own virtue. And as injustice, whether by fraud or force, would be unknown among themselves, so they would be sufficiently secured from it in their neighbours. For cunning and false self-interest, confederacies in injustice . . . . would be found mere childish folly and weakness when set in opposition against wisdom, public spirit, union inviolable, and fidelity—allowing both a sufficient length of years to try their force. Add the general influence which such a kingdom would have over the face of the earth, by way of example particularly, and the reverence which would be paid it. It would plainly be superior to all others, and the world must gradually come under its empire . . . . The head of it would be a universal monarch, in another sense than any mortal has yet been, and the Eastern style would be literally applicable to him, that 'all people, nations, and languages should serve him.' And though indeed our knowledge of human nature, and the whole history of mankind, show the impossibility without some miraculous interposition that a number of men should unite here on earth in one society or government, in the fear of God and universal practice of virtue, and that such a government should continue so united for a succession of ages, yet admitting or supposing this, the effect would be as now drawn out. And thus, for instance, the wonderful power and prosperity promised to the Jewish nation in the Scripture would be in great measure the consequence of what is predicted of them, that 'the people should be all righteous, and inherit the land for ever' (Isai. 60. 21)."

Other questions relating, *e.g.* to Antichrist, seem hardly ready for solution, in spite of all the light thrown on them by past and present history. We have to keep our minds in suspense, but also on the alert. If there were many antichrists in St. John's time, how many must there be now! and how many "men of sin!" Yet this need not hinder us from a strong expectation that a wicked one has yet to be revealed

Antichrist.

who will become an embodiment of many kinds of iniquity, superstition, and oppression.

Times of the Gentiles. It is curious to notice how deeply some traditional impression concerning the future roots itself in the convictions of those who have not the means or will not take the trouble to search out the evidence on the subject. Thus, in the early Church, the period of the outbreak after the Millennium was generally fixed at three and a half years. So now many have jumped to the conclusion that "the times of the Gentiles" are 2,520 years, *i.e.* 360 × 7, or seven prophetic years.* This theory has no real foundation in Scripture. It cannot be gathered from the "seven-times" of Lev. **26.** 18, which speaks of a sevenfold punishment threatened to sinful Israel. Still less can it be gathered from the "seven times" of Nebuchadnezzar's punishment (Dan. **4.** 32), which cannot be made to prefigure either good times for the Gentiles, or oppressive times for Israel. Shall we then take refuge in the fact that 2,520 is the least common multiple of the first ten numerals? or that this number yields a period of seventy-five years' difference between the amount of solar and lunar years? These can hardly be called sober and reasonable interpretations. We have full conviction that there is a timing of events in the heavens with great and vital transactions on earth, but we must not let our love of figures run away with principles of sound interpretation. But this idea of 2,520 having once got into the mind, is not easily got rid of. It becomes a measure for the sacred calendar of prophecy, and beguiles students into fixing a starting point, a mid-way era, and a closing crisis for the times of the Gentiles. These "times" are accordingly made to rise with the era of Nabonassar (B.C. 747), which was about coeval with the earliest attacks

---

* See Elliott's *Horæ Apoc.*, vi. 5. 1.

CONCLUDING OBSERVATIONS. 177

on Israel by the Assyrian kings. They close in the days of Louis XVI., when the French Revolution was approaching; or they may be made to begin seventy-five years later, in B.C. 598, when Nebuchadnezzar took Jerusalem, and to close in about A.D. 1848. In the one case the bisecting line takes us to the overthrow of the Western Roman Empire (circ. 476), in the other to A.D. 663.* This method of dealing with figures may sometimes bring out interesting results, but it is to be received with considerable hesitation. The caution of some of the ante-Nicene expositors, and of such later students as Pusey and Birks, is by all means to be imitated.

No better words can be found to close the present volume than those uttered in 1879 by that veteran student of prophecy, Dr. Horatius Bonar, and published in the *Missing Link Magazine* for May in that year. He says :— *Dr. Bonar on Prophecy.*

"I speak my own experience in this matter, and I compromise no one in saying what I do except myself—I say I am getting, after fifty years' study, greatly more certain, and I am getting greatly more uncertain, about many things in the prophetic word; allow me as briefly as possible to tell you both my certainties and my uncertainties, and you will see how strictly they bear upon what I have to say concerning the Master's testimony.

"I feel greatly more certain as to the *second coming* of the Lord being the Church's hope. That is the first thing. I feel greatly more certain, as the years roll on, regarding the *pre-millennial advent*. I feel greatly more certain concerning the first resurrection and the millennial reign. I feel greatly more certain concerning the times of the restitution of all things spoken of by all the holy prophets since the world began. I feel greatly more certain concerning the new

---

* See Guinness's Appendix to his *Approaching End of the Age*.

heaven and the new earth wherein dwelleth righteousness. I feel greatly more certain in reference to *Israel's* prospects of glory in the latter day, after their scattering of 1800 years. I feel greatly more certain in reference to the *doom of antichrist*, whatever that name may include, and doubtless it includes many things. So regarding these things that I have thus briefly enumerated, and on which I should have liked to dwell, I would say I feel the power of a demonstration now. They form part of what appears to me a demonstrative creed.

"But then, on the other hand, there are things regarding which I am more uncertain than I used to be, for I thought some forty or fifty years ago that I had settled a great many of the prophetic questions which have now come to be unsettled. I feel uncertain, very uncertain, as to the prophetical *dates*—I confess that, and I confess also that I have given up many of those dates that I once thought I could have reckoned on. I feel more uncertain in reference to the *Apocalypse*—I confess that. I do not adhere, I may say, to any of the different schools. I profess to be a learner still in regard to the Apocalypse, and I am waiting for light; and I believe the Holy Spirit will give it, and that we shall ere long, it may be, understand that marvellous book which the Church has been, age after age, trying to comprehend, but which, I believe, it has hitherto failed in a great measure to unravel. I feel also uncertain as to the details of events and the relations of events, especially regarding *Israel's* latter-day history. It is not that I do not believe every word that is written concerning Israel in the latter day, but I feel at a loss how to arrange the various things which at first sight seem to conflict the one with the other. And I feel, I confess, very uncertain as to the personalites, or to the personages, and positions and relations of the following names or *nationalities* which figure in the prophetic word—*Babylon*, Assyria, Edom, Elam, Egypt, Moab, Ammon, Gog, and Magog. God has something in the future of all these, but I confess I stop there, I am not able to say more or to arrange the future of these, but there I leave them, and I am quite sure that ere long we shall get light upon them, and that the event will prove that in regard to every one of these the Holy Spirit had a special meaning in what He has written concerning them in the prophetic word.

"Let these things suffice, brethren—perhaps they are too brief—to let you know something of my own experience in reference to the greater certainties and the greater uncertainties that have passed through my own mind during these many years since I began to study the prophetic word.

"There is just one thing in connexion with this matter that I should like to add, and it is with regard to the certainties, for it applies to the whole, and I should like to avow it solemnly in these days. *I feel a vastly greater certainty in reference to the Divine authority and verbal inspiration of the Word of God.* If ever a doubt passed through my mind during the last fifty years in reference to these, that doubt has disappeared. And then, in connexion with this, I feel a greater certainty as to the literal interpretation of that whole Word of God—historical, doctrinal, prophetical. 'Literal, if possible,' is, I believe, the only maxim that will carry you right through the Word of God from Genesis to Revelation."

LEADING DATES REFERRED TO IN DISCUSSIONS ON PROPHECY.

	B.C.
Era of Nabonassar	747
Capture of Samaria	722–1
Three captures of Jerusalem, by Nebuchadnezzar	606–5 / 598–7 / 588–7
Capture of Babylon	539–8
First return of Jews	536
Temple rebuilt	521–15
Ahasuerus (Xerxes)	485
Artaxerxes Longimanus	465–4
Ezra's commission	458–7
Nehemiah's commission	445–4
Alexander the Great visits Jerusalem	332
Ptolemy Soter visits Jerusalem	320
Era of the Seleucidæ	312
Antiochus Epiphanes	175
Jerusalem defiled	169
Rome conquers Macedonia	166
Cleansing of the Temple	165
Capture of Jerusalem by Pompey	63
Crassus plunders the Temple	51
Herod king of Judea	40
,, captures Jerusalem	37
Augustus emperor	27
Herod begins to restore the Temple	19

	B.C.
Birth of the Lord Jesus	5–3
Herod dies	4–3

	A.D.
Tiberius emperor	14
Pilate procurator	26
Death, Resurrection, and Ascension of the Lord Jesus	29–34
Jewish war begins (12th year of Nero). St. Paul martyred same year	66
Capture of Jerusalem by Titus	70
Domitian banishes John to Patmos	95
Revolt under Bar-Cochab	130
Jews banished from Jerusalem	134
Decius	249–51
Diocletian	284–305
Constantine	306–37
Julian the Apostate	361–3
Papal jurisdiction over the West granted by Gratian and Valentinian II.	378–9
Break up of Western Roman Empire from Honorius to Romulus Augustulus, with corresponding increase of Papacy	395–475

DATES REFERRED TO IN DISCUSSIONS ON PROPHECY.

	A.D.
Edict of Justinian I. to Pope John, "Head of all the churches"	533
Decree of Emperor Phocus giving Pope Boniface III. title of Universal Pastor	608
Rise of Islam	622
Jerusalem captured by Omar	636
Ravenna given to the Pope by Pepin	755
Lombardy added	774
Rome (city and duchy) added by Charlemagne	799
Charlemagne crowned by Pope Leo III.	800
Constantinople taken by Turks	1453
Reformation (Diet of Worms)	1521
French Revolution	1782-3
Temporal power of the Pope overthrown	1866-70

INDEX OF NAMES AND SUBJECTS.

	PAGE
Advent of Christ, pre-millennial	146
——, its spiritual influence	172
Anderson, Dr., on Daniel	102
Anglo-Israel theory	133
Antichrist	151
Antiochus Epiphanes	157
Apocalypse, structure of	110
——, author of	112
Arnold, Dr., on prophecy	73
Arthur's "Tongue of Fire"	147
Attributes of God involved in prophecy	3
Augustine	146, 158
Babylon	156
Bacon, Lord, on prophecy	xiii
Barron on the Jew	128
Birks' Outlines	x, 114
Blessing promised to Abraham	116
Body, spiritual	165
Bonaparte	vii
Bonar, Horatius, on prophecy	177
Branch, the	83
Butler, Bishop, on the future	174
Call of the prophets	41
Canaan	115
Captivity, turning of	57
Celsus	157
Chain of prophets	44
Chapters, special	108
Chronological prophecies	89

	PAGE
Church	87
Coming of the Lord	56
Compass, points of	52
Conditional prophecies	25
Creation	66
Darkness	50
David	71
David, Son of	73, 120
Davison on prophecy	viii
Day of the Lord	55
Dead, state of	159
Deluge	67
Earth, the new	49, 147, 164, 168
Earthquakes	49
Egypt	68
Elijah	69
Elliott, E. B.	ix, 110
Equity	161
Exodus	68
Faber on prophecy	vi
Fairbairn on prophecy	ix
Figurative language	48
Fire	51, 67
Firstfruits	78
Fleming on prophecy	ix
Foreground in prophecy	21
Foresight	33
Formulæ in prophecy	54
Frere on prophecy	vi, ix

INDEX OF NAMES AND SUBJECTS.

	PAGE
Garratt on prophecy	x., 110
Gibbon's History	172
Giffard on prophecy	x
Girdlestone, Wm., on Daniel	103
Glory of God	64
Gnosticism	151
Guinness	x, 110
Hebrew names of prophets	34
Hippolytus	95, 157
Horsley, Bishop	ix
Ideal prophecies	1
Inspiration	33
Intermediate state	163
Interpretation of Scripture	80
Irenæus	148, 157
Irving, Edward	x
Israel	87, 125, 134
Judgment	160
Justin Martyr	148
Kingdom of God	63
„ of David	72
Lactantius	157
Lacunza	x
Last days	54
Levitical system	76
Louis, Pierre	vi
Margoliouth, Professor	xii
Marriage	52
Messiah	120, 122
Millennium	95, 141, 143
Mohammedanism	vii, 153
Names	81
Nations, all	59, 116

	PAGE
Nazarene	83
Newton, Bishop	ix
„ Sir Isaac	ix
Numbers	89
Offerings, typical	78
Origen	157
Outbreak, the final	148
Papias	148
Paradise	66
Parousia	56, 141, 156
Persecuting Emperors	158
Porter, Professor	xi
Priests	77
Prophecies, their number	8
——, —— variety	8
——, —— characteristics	9
——, —— relationship	10
——, —— effects	12
——, —— fulfilment	16
——, —— tests	17
Prophets, groups of	105
Punishment of the lost	164
Pusey, Dr.	x
Quotations	84
Remnant, the	58, 126
Repentance	25
Resurrection	163, 165
Retribution	161
Revelation	2
Romanism	vii, 153
Sand	50
Satan	150
Schools of prophetic study	110
Sea	50
Seed of Abraham	116
Seven	111

INDEX OF NAMES AND SUBJECTS.

	PAGE
Shiloh	96
Social position of prophets	37
Sodom	67
Smith, Alder	xi
Smith, Payne-	x
Spirit, gift of	116, 117
Stanton, Professor	x
Tabernacle	61, 77
Taylor, Isaac	x, 168
Tertullian	158
Times of the Gentiles	176
Trench on prophecy	x

	PAGE
Tribes, the ten	125
—— never "lost"	126
—— reunited	129
Unconditional prophecy	
"Unseen Universe"	x, 168
Varieties in destiny	162
Victorinus	158
Visions	36
World, end of	62
Year, Jewish	101

INDEX OF TEXTS.

GENESIS.

	PAGE
1. 14	19
2—9.	44
2. 8	66
2. 17	15, 28
2. 21	32
3. 15	115
4. 15	111
5. 29	81
6. 3	89, 117
6. 13	62, 118
8. 22	30
10. 32	59
11—50.	44
12.	108
12. 1	49
12. 3	59, 116
13. 14–17	90
15. 5	50
15. 8	19
15. 12	32
15. 13	90
17. 4	60
17. 5	81
18. 18	59
19. 24	67
19. 28	68
22. 17, 18	50, 59, 116
25. 22	45
28. 3	61
35. 11	116
37. 9	154
41. 45	41
45. 7	41, 58
48. 4	61, 116
49.	108
49. 1	54
49. 10	96
50. 20	41

EXODUS.

	PAGE
2. 10	81
3. 7	62
3. 12	20
4. 15, 16	34
6. 7	54
7. 1	34
12. 40	90
15. 2	69
15. 18	63
16. 6, 7	64
16. 12	54
17. 15	45
21. 6	14
23. 19	79
24. 11	35
24. 16, 17	64
25. 9, 40	77
29. 42, 45	61
35. 22	129
37. 23	111

LEVITICUS.

	PAGE
2. 12, 14	79
16.	78
23.	78
23. 15, 16	79
25. 10	57
26.	11, 25, 106, 108, 128
26. 11, 12	62
26. 18	92, 111, 176
26. 34, 35	92

NUMBERS.

	PAGE
3. 7. 8	77
12. 6, 8	35
14. 33	91
14. 34	28
16. 22	118
23. 10	62
23. 19	28
24. 4	35
24. 14	54
28. 26	79

DEUTERONOMY.

	PAGE
1. 7, 8	115
1. 10	50, 116
4. 26	15
4. 30	54
8. 13	68
9. 3, 6	51, 68
10. 22	116
11. 5	68
11. 24, 30	115
13. 1–3	23
26—29.	11, 128
28.	68, 108
28. 1	60
28. 41	57
28. 62	67
29. 23	67
30. 1–3	60
30. 3	57
31. 29	54
32.	11, 108, 135
32. 8	59
32. 43	119

INDEX OF TEXTS.

JOSHUA.
	PAGE
5. 14	45
6. 4	111
6. 5	91
6. 27	45

JUDGES.
1. 1	45
2. 1, 20	45
5. 14	10
6. 8	45
7. 12	50
10. 11	45
13. 6	45
18. 5	45
20. 18–27	45

1 SAMUEL.
2. 27	45
3.	45
9. 9	34
10. 5	32
12. 12	63
15. 29	28
15. 35	28
19. 20	31

2 SAMUEL.
5. 20, 25	69
7.	71, 120
22. 50	119
24. 11	35

1 KINGS.
4. 3	10
4. 20	50, 116
4. 21, 24	50, 115
6. 13	61
8. 27	61
11. 29	46
12. 15	46
13.	19, 46
15. 29	46
16.	97
16. 1, 7, 12	46
20. 13–23	46
20. 28	46, 54
20. 35	31, 46
21. 27–29	27
22. 8	46
22. 19	36

2 KINGS.
2. 3	31
3. 15	32
4. 38	31
9. 1	31
10. 30	46
14. 25	46, 95
15. 12	46
15. 29	125
17. 3–6	126
17. 24	126
18. 10–12	126
19. 4	58
20. 4	35
20. 6	91
21. 14	58

1 CHRONICLES.
2. 55	10
9. 1, 2	128
12.	127
17.	71, 120
22. 9	83
25. 1	32
28. 12, 19	77
29. 29	35, 45

2 CHRONICLES.
9. 29	45
12. 15	45
15. 1, 8	46
20. 14	46
20. 34	46
20. 37	46
21. 12	46
23. 2	127
24. 5, 16	127
24. 19, 20	46
25. 7, 15	46
26. 5	46
26. 22	46
28.	97
28. 9	46
28. 23	127
29. 25	45
30, 31.	126
32. 32	46
33. 11	42
33. 19	46
34. 6–9	127
34. 33	127
35. 2, 18	127
35. 25	46
36. 12, 21	46, 92

EZRA.
6. 17–21	128
7. 10	128
8. 35	128
9. 1	128
10. 5, 23	128

NEHEMIAH.
2.	94
9. 30	34
11. 20	59, 128

PSALMS.
2. 4, 6	29
11. 6	67
14. 7	57
18. 49	119
22. 27	60
47. 8	119
49. 4	32

		PAGE			PAGE			PAGE
53. 6	. .	57	10. 20–24	.	132	40. 3	. .	70
65. 2	. .	118	10. 21, 22	.	58, 82	40. 5, 6	.	64, 118
67. 2	. .	119	11. 10	.	71, 119	40. 10	. .	56
72. 8	. .	50	11. 15	. .	69	41. 22, 23	. .	3
72. 11	.	60, 119	12. 2	. .	69	42. 1, 6	.	119
72. 17	. .	60	13. 1	. .	36	43.	. . .	69
85. 1	. .	57	13. 6	. .	55	44. 3	. .	117
86. 9	.	60, 119	13. 9	. .	55	45. 25	. .	82
89.	. .	71, 72	13. 10	. .	51	46. 9–11	. .	3
89. 29, 36, 37	.	30	13. 13	. .	49	46. 13	. .	82
90. 4	. .	95	13, 14.	.	109	49. 6	. .	119
104. 30	. .	66	14.	. .	150	51. 3	. .	66
110. 4	. .	29	16. 5	. .	72	52. 15	. .	60
126. 1, 4	.	57	16. 14	. .	91	53.	. .	109
132.	. . .	71	19.	. .	57	54. 9	. .	67
			20. 3	. .	91	55. 3	. .	72
ISAIAH.			21. 16	. .	91	56. 7	. .	79
1. 7–23	. .	14	22. 15	.	21, 71	58. 1	. .	125
1. 9, 10	. .	67	23. 15–17	.	91	59. 19–21	.	117
1. 26	. .	83	24.	. .	49	59. 20	. .	56
1. 31	. .	52	24—27.	.	109	60. 7	. .	79
2. 2	. 55, 60, 119	24. 18–20	.	13	60. 19, 20	.	51
2. 12	. .	55	24. 19	. .	49	60. 21	. .	175
4. 5	. .	69	24. 21	. .	57	61. 1	. .	117
6.	. .	xii	24. 23	. .	63	61. 1, 2	.	58
6. 5	. .	63	26. 21	. .	56	62. 4	. .	83
6. 13	. .	59	27. 12	. .	69	64.	. . .	69
7. 3	.	58, 82	27. 13	.	58, 69	65. 17	.	30, 65
7. 8	. .	91	28. 7	. .	23	66. 18, 20	.	60
7. 14	.	21, 82	28. 21	. .	69	66. 20–22	30, 66, 79
7. 16	.	82, 97	28. 29	. .	82	66. 24	. .	52
8. 3	. .	38	30. 10	. .	35			
8. 4	. .	97	30. 26	. .	51	**JEREMIAH.**		
8. 7	. .	50	32. 14	. .	14	2. 8	. .	23
8. 8, 10	. .	82	32. 15	. .	117	3. 6–22	.	129
8. 14	. .	125	34. 4	. .	51	3. 12	. .	26
8. 18	. .	82	35.	. .	69	4. 4	. .	52
8. 20	. .	24	35. 2	. .	64	6. 26	. .	48
8. 22	. .	51	35. 8	. .	83	7. 31–33	.	164
9. 1	. .	126	36. 3	. .	21	16. 14, 15	.	68
9. 6, 7	71, 82, 142	38. 12	. .	83	18. 7–10	.	26
10. 6, 7	. .	6	40—66.	.	132	20. 9	. .	36

INDEX OF TEXTS.

	PAGE
23. 5	72
23. 6	82
23. 14	67
25. 11, 12	92
26. 12, 13	26
26. 17-19	13
26. 18	98
28. 9	16
28. 16, 17	21
29. 10	92
30. 1-9	130
30. 3	57
30. 9	72
31.	130
31. 31-34	131
32. 27	118
33.	130
33. 18	79
33. 19-26	30
33. 24	125
38. 17, 18	25
42. 10-13	25
46. 10	52
48. 47	55, 57
49. 6	57
49. 39	55
50. 4, 5	130
50. 9	52
51. 5	130
51. 42	50

EZEKIEL.

4. 4-9	93
5.	59
7. 2	62
8. 3	48
13. 5	55
16. 49, 53	67
18. 30-32	27
21. 27	97
26. 7	52
29. 11-13	92

	PAGE
29. 14	57
30. 3	55
32. 7	51
32. 30	52
33.	26
33. 13-15	27
34. 23	131
34. 23, 24	72
35. 10	125
37.	128, 131
37. 22-25	72
37. 26, 27, 28	61, 62
38.	52, 144
38, 39.	52, 109, 150
38. 6, 15	52
38. 8, 16	55
38. 22	67
39. 25	57
40—48	36
43. 19	79
44. 15	79
47. 13	131

DANIEL.

2.	99, 109
4. 16, 23, 25, 32	92
4. 32	176
6. 25	60
7.	109
7, 8, 11	150
7. 14	60, 64
7. 18, 27	64
7. 22	146
7. 25	92, 101
8. 14	93, 99
9.	94, 109, 141
9. 1	92
9. 25	57
10, 11.	107
10. 2	94
10. 14	55
11. 6-40	52

	PAGE
11. 21	153
11. 31, 35	153
11. 37	152
12. 7	92, 101
12. 8, 13	38
12. 11, 12	93
12. 13	63

HOSEA.

1. 1	95
1. 2	36, 52
1. 4-9	83
1. 6, 11	127-9
1. 10	50
2. 15	69
2. 16	83
3. 5	55, 57, 72, 129
4. 15	127
6. 2	71, 95
6. 11	57
8. 13	68
9. 3, 6	68
9. 9	69
10. 9	69
11. 1	95
11. 5	68
11. 8	129
14. 4	129

JOEL.

1 15	55
2.	38
2. 1	55
2. 10	51
2. 28	98, 118
2. 27	132
2. 31	51, 70
3. 1	57
3. 2, 12	60
3. 15	51
3. 17	54

INDEX OF TEXTS.

AMOS.

	PAGE
2. 4, 6	127
3. 7	3
3. 8	39
4. 10, 11	68
5. 3	59
5. 4	129
5. 8	111
5. 18	55
9. 8	98
9. 11	72
9. 11, 12	145
9. 14	57

OBADIAH.

17.	125
21.	63

JONAH.

3. 4	91

MICAH.

3. 9	125
3. 11	23
3. 12	98
4, 5.	22
4. 1	55, 98
4. 7	63
5. 2	98
5. 3	111
7. 20	98

ZEPHANIAH.

1. 7, 14, 18	55
2. 13	52
3. 13-15	132

HAGGAI.

2.	71
2. 6	50
3. 21	50

ZECHARIAH.

	PAGE
1. 17	67
2. 10, 11	60, 61
3.	71
3. 9	111
4. 2	111
4. 4-7	38
4. 14	87
6. 1-4	87
7. 12	34
8. 3	61, 83
8. 13	132
9. 10	50, 119
10. 10, 11	69
12—14.	109
12. 7-10	72
14. 1	55
14. 4	50

MALACHI.

1. 1	36
1. 4	83
1. 7	79
1. 11	79, 119
3. 1	70
3. 2	52, 56
3. 3	79
4. 1	52
4. 5	70, 98

ST. MATTHEW.

1. 12	75
1. 18-25	82
1. 20	73, 120
2. 15	95
3. 12	52
7. 16	24
7. 22	57
8. 11	119
9. 36	xi
10. 6	xi, 131
10. 15	67, 161
11. 14	70
11. 22, 24	161
11. 24	67
11. 28, 29	97
12. 29	146
12. 40	95
12. 41, 42	161
13.	135
13. 39, 40, 49	63
19. 28	146
21. 42	119
23. 32	90
24.	22, 56, 62, 99, 109, 135
24. 3	39, 63
24. 14, 15	23, 60, 94, 140
24. 29	51
25.	22, 60, 109
25. 32	60
25. 46	163
26. 13	140
28. 19	140
28. 20	63

ST. MARK.

1. 15	94
13.	99, 135
16. 15	13, 140

ST. LUKE.

1. 26-37	73, 82, 120
1. 32, 33	72, 74
1. 32, 35	82
1. 33	143, 145
1. 55, 70	116
1. 60	83
1. 69	74, 120
1. 72, 73	83
2. 1	140
2. 32	116, 119, 145
3. 23	74
11. 50, 51	40

INDEX OF TEXTS.

	PAGE
12. 39	56
21.	99, 135
21. 20	94
21. 24	60, 99
21. 32	99
21. 34	56
22. 30	131
24.	118
24. 26, 46	39
24. 27, 45	84
24. 49	117

ST. JOHN.

1. 14	61, 65
5. 24	146
6. 39–54	55
7. 37–39	117
8. 46	24
11. 40	65
12. 24	165
13. 19	16
14.	118
14. 2, 3	138, 165
14. 9, 12	65
14. 29	16
15. 26	117
19. 39	168

ACTS.

1.	118
1. 4	117
1. 6, 7	39, 58, 136, 137
2.	38
2. 5	60
2. 7–11	128
2. 23	6
2. 30	45, 74
2. 33	118
3. 13	65
3. 17, 18	2
3. 19, 20	100, 139
3. 21	58, 104

	PAGE
3. 25. 26	59, 116
7. 6, 7	90
10. 38	117
11. 5	32
11. 28	140
13. 22	73, 74
13. 27	2
13. 47	119
14. 15	37
15. 16, 17	98, 145
15. 18	5
17. 26	59
20. 29, 30	151
22. 17	32
26. 7	131
27. 20	51
27. 25	17

ROMANS.

1. 3	74
2. 4	26
2. 28, 29	88
8. 19	142
8. 21	169
9—11	109, 139
9. 27	59
10. 18	137
11. 5	59
11. 15	63
11. 25	100, 139
11. 26	139, 145
11. 29	29
12. 1	80
15. 9, 10	119
15. 16	80

1 CORINTHIANS.

1. 8	55
3. 13–15	142
5. 5	55
6. 2	146
13. 12	54, 172
14. 32	32, 38

	PAGE
15.	9, 148
15. 22	142
15. 23	79, 100
15. 24	63
15. 28	145
15. 35	165

2 CORINTHIANS.

1. 14	55
3. 16	139
5. 10	163
6. 16	62
12. 2	32

GALATIANS.

1. 15	42
3. 17	90
4. 4	94

EPHESIANS.

1. 13	117
2. 19–22	114

PHILIPPIANS.

3. 20, 21	142, 167

COLOSSIANS.

1. 6	137, 140
1. 23	13, 137, 140
1. 28	162
3. 4	142

1 THESS.

2. 19	142
4. 14–17	100
5. 2, 4	56

2 THESS.

1. 6–9	100, 163
1. 7	142
2.	96, 151, 156
2. 2	100
2. 3, 4, 5	154
2. 8–11	154

2 TIMOTHY.

	PAGE
2. 11, 12	. 142
2. 20	. . 163
3. 1	. . . 55
4. 1, 8	. 142, 162
4. 17	. . 140

HEBREWS.

1. 1	. . . 34
7. 14	. . . 74
8. 4, 5	. . . 77
8. 8–12	. . 132
9. 26, 28	56, 63, 145
11. 12	. . . 50
11. 30	. . . 111
12. 26-28	. . 50
12. 29	. . . 51
13. 15, 16	. . 80

ST. JAMES.

1. 1	. . . 131
1. 12	. . . 162
5. 3	. . . 55
5. 17	. . . 37

1 PETER.

1. 4	. . . 169
1. 7	. . . 52
1. 10–12	. 38, 107
2. 4–10	. . 111
2. 5	. . . 80
3. 20	. . . 89
4. 5	. . . 142
5. 4	. . . 162

2 PETER.

1. 19	. . . 171
1. 21	. . 32, 34
2. 1–3	. . . 151

	PAGE
2. 5, 6	. . . 67
3. 3	. . 24, 55
3. 5	. . . 67
3. 7, 12	. . 52
3. 8	. . . 95
3. 9	. . . 27
3. 10	. . . 56
3. 13	. . 30, 66

1 JOHN.

2. 18	. . . 151
2. 27	. . . 118
3. 2	. . . 142
4. 1–3	. 24, 151

ST. JUDE.

7.	 68
14.	 56
18.	 24

REVELATION.

1—22.	. . . 36
1. 1–3	. . 112
1. 3	. . . 171
1. 6	. . . 80
1. 7	. . . 144
2. 7	. . . 67
2. 25	. . . 144
3. 3	. . . 56
3. 7	. . . 71
3. 11	. . 56, 144
3. 21	. . . 144
5. 5	. . 74, 97
6. 1–8	. . . 87
6. 12	. . . 51
7. 13, 14	. . 38
10. 4	. . . 113
11.	. . . 101

	PAGE
11. 2	. . 93, 113
11. 3	. . . 93
11. 4	. . . 87
11. 8	. . . 67
11. 15	. 113, 144
12.	. . 101, 113
12. 5	. . . 156
12. 14	. . . 93
13.	. . . 113
14. 1–13	. . 113
14. 14—19. 21	. 113
14. 11	. . . 67
16. 15	. . . 56
17. 15, 18	. . 156
19. 7–9	. . . 53
19. 10	. . . 10
19. 15–21	. . 156
19. 17, 18	. . 52
19. 20	. . . 67
20.	9, 109, 143, 144,
	145, 146, 156
20. 1–10	. . 113
20. 2–7	. . . 95
20. 8	. . . 52
21.	. . 109, 169
21. 1	. 30, 50, 66
21. 2	. . . 53
21. 3	. . . 61
21. 9	. . . 53
21. 20	. . . 51
21. 24	. . . 114
21. 27	. . . 114
22.	. . 109, 169
22. 1, 2	. . . 67
22. 5	. . . 51
22. 6, 7	. 56, 112
22. 15	. . . 114
22. 16	. . 72, 74
22. 20	. . 56, 115

www.ingramcontent.com/pod-product-compliance
Lightning Source LLC
Chambersburg PA
CBHW051923160426
43198CB00012B/2018